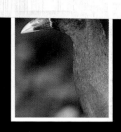

# BIRDS
*in*
## FOCUS

# BIRDS
*in*
## FOCUS

MARK CARWARDINE

*Foreword by*
DAVID BELLAMY

**Longmeadow Press**

FOR ADAM, VANESSA AND JESSICA

This 1990 edition is published by
Longmeadow Press
201 High Ridge Road
Stamford, CT 06904

ISBN: 0-681-40985-1

0 9 8 7 6 5 4 3 2 1

CREDITS
Editing/Picture Research: Krystyna Mayer
Design: Peter Bridgewater/Stuart Walden
Colour Reproduction: Scantrans Pte, Ltd., Singapore
Printed in Singapore

# Contents

# FOREWORD

. . . . . . . . . . . . . . . . . .

THIS IS A TIMELY BOOK, published as the last decade of a century which has seen so much destruction breathes hope for a more enlightened future. It is the decade of reconstruction.

I am writing this foreword in New Zealand, home to some of the world's rarest and most extraordinary birds. They are seriously threatened by habitat destruction and the introduction of mammals, but I am glad to report that, on many fronts, the bird experts here are winning. That is what I like about this book — it is not a catalogue of doom, but one of hope. Above all, it is a celebration of the beauty and wonder of birds, with words of warning wherever we are pushing a species

towards extinction. It should inspire us all to take steps to rectify the damage we have done.

Mark is a tireless campaigner for conservation. Since we first met in Madagascar, once home to some of the largest birds ever to have lived on earth, I have been privileged to work with him over the years. Only last year, we stood and marvelled together at the gigantic populations of little auks on Spitzbergen and Jan Mayen, in the Arctic.

We are, indeed, fortunate people to be able to see some of these sights for ourselves, so it's great to be able to share some of that experience with you through the pages of this book. Please heed the warnings and work with us to turn the tide of reconstruction. It is our last chance.

*David Bellamy*

**David Bellamy**

**AUCKLAND, FEBRUARY 1990**

**PYGMY KINGFISHER**
*(Ceyx picta)* ABOVE LEFT

**OSTRICH**
*(Struthio camelus)* LEFT

**RED-CRESTED TURACO**
*(Tauraco erythrolphus)* ABOVE RIGHT

**CORAL-BILLED GROUND CUCKOO**
*(Carpococcyx renauldi)* ABOVE

**KING EIDER**
*(Somateria spectabilis)* LEFT

**BATELEUR EAGLE**
*(Terathopius ecaudatus)* OPPOSITE

# INTRODUCTION

. . . . . . . . . . . . . . . . .

**BEWICK'S SWAN**
*(Cygnus bewickii)*

150 MILLION YEARS AGO a strange creature launched itself from a tree and began to glide through its prehistoric woodland home. The animal was an *Archaeopteryx*, or 'ancient bird', and it was probably the first bird to inhabit the earth.

The size of a crow, *Archaeopteryx* differed substantially from the birds of today. It was an intriguing middle stage between the dinosaurs (from which it is believed to have descended) and modern birds. It had a long, bony tail, jaws lined with teeth, a relatively small breastbone, claws on the 'fingers' of its wings – and feathers.

All birds, without exception, have feathers and no other member of the animal kingdom has them. Feathers are made largely from a tough protein called keratin, which also forms rhino horn, human fingernails and claws. They probably evolved as a form of insulation from reptile scales, which are made of the same substance.

A single bird has between 1,000 and 25,000 feathers, depending on the species. They are crucial to its survival, providing everything from waterproofing to camouflage. Some feathers are soft and downy for trapping a layer of air to keep the bird warm; some are body feathers and provide streamlining; wing feathers are used mainly in flight; and tail feathers are used for display, balance, steering and braking.

*Archaeopteryx* did not have the enormous wing muscles necessary for powered flight. It clambered about in the trees and glided from branch to branch, but was probably never able to fly with anything other than weak wingbeats. With some exceptions, modern birds have powerful muscles anchored to a huge projection of the breastbone, called the keel. These enable them to flap their wings and make them the most highly mobile animals in the world.

Birds occupy almost every corner of our planet. They have penetrated to within a short distance of the two Poles, and live in deserts and oceans, cities and jungles. The emperor penguin can dive to a depth of 870 ft (265 m) and large birds of prey are frequently seen from aeroplanes. A Ruppell's vulture once collided with a plane over the Ivory Coast, West Africa, at a height of 37,000 ft (11,277 m).

To survive in such extremes, birds must be able to cope with freezing cold, scorching heat, gale-force winds, pouring rain, rough seas, blinding snowstorms and torrential currents. Emperor penguins are adapted to incubating their eggs at the coldest place on earth — on the Antarctic ice-cap in mid-winter. They huddle together to keep warm and their short, fine feathers are devoted entirely to insulation. Brave torrent ducks, which live in the fast-flowing rivers of the Andes, spend most of their lives battling against the swirling whitewaters in search of food. Their webbed feet are so enormous that their eggs have to be specially big for them to fit inside.

Birds rely on the help of such special adaptations, and these can apply to their behaviour, physiology, feathers, wings, feet and bills. The macaw's bill is large and powerful for cracking open nuts; the eagle's is hooked for tearing flesh; the nightjar's is wide for catching insects in flight; and the hummingbird has a long, thin bill for sucking nectar out of flowers.

**AFRICAN JACANA**
*(Actophilornis africanus)*

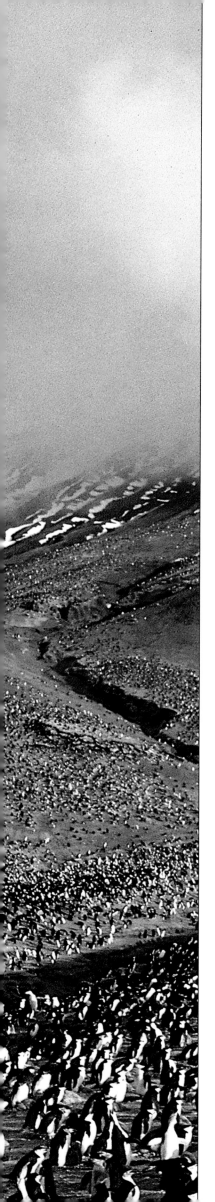

**MUTE SWAN**
*(Cygnus olor)* ABOVE

**CHINSTRAP PENGUIN**
*(Pygoscelis antarctica)* LEFT

With so many different adaptations, it is not surprising that birds come in such a breathtaking variety of shapes, sizes and colours. There are nearly 9,000 species altogether – more than twice as many birds as there are mammals. At one extreme is the tiny bee hummingbird, less than 2.5 in (6 cm) in length and dwarfed in its rain forest home by some butterflies. At the other is the ostrich, which reaches a height of 9 ft (2.7 m) and weighs far more than a man.

Many birds have learnt to live in close proximity to people and are turning radical changes in the environment to their advantage. Magpies are experts at dodging the traffic on busy motorways; snowy owls assemble around airport runways to hunt rodents; and black kites have become the ultimate urban rag-pickers.

But many other birds have succumbed to the pressures of environmental degradation. During the past 600 years we have lost nearly 150 birds, and many more have probably disappeared even before we were aware of their existence. The great auk, dodo, Colombian grebe, laughing owl, glaucous macaw, Tahiti sandpiper and pink-headed duck were among them. Even the passenger pigeon, which was probably the commonest bird that ever lived on earth, has gone. Enormous flocks, covering areas that could be measured in miles, darkened the sky and were common sight

in North America in the early 1800s. Yet people managed to hunt the species to extinction within just 50 years.

Today, more than 1,000 birds are nearing extinction. Many are so rare that only a handful are left and they are unlikely to survive for much longer without vigorous action to save them. In New Zealand, the kakapo is down to just 43 birds; the Madagascar serpent eagle has been seen only once or twice in the past 50 years; and in Mauritius, the echo parakeet is down to the last 14 individuals.

Extinction is a natural and continuous process of evolution and birds have been becoming extinct for millions of years. At least 90 per cent of all species that have ever existed have disappeared. But in comparatively recent times, with the advent of hunting, egg collecting, pollution, the introduction of exotic predators and, most important of all, habitat destruction, the extinction rate has soared. The destruction of rain forests alone has reached staggering proportions – and they are home to more than one in three of the world's birds.

As human numbers increase, even greater pressures will be placed on the environment. More habitats will disappear and the extinction rate will continue to soar. We are responsible for this proliferating destruction, yet we possess the power and the knowledge to take action to do something about it. Many of the birds in this book are relying on that action for their survival.

**FORK-TAILED SUNBIRD**
*(Aethopyga christinae)*

# CHAPTER ONE

# MASTERS OF THE AIR

**EAGLE OWL**
*(Bubo bubo)*

**B**IRDS ARE SUCCESSFUL *because they are able to fly. They can escape from ground-dwelling predators, obtain food that is beyond the reach of other animals and travel extremely long distances to take advantage of seasonally abundant food supplies on offer in many different parts of the world.*

*Nearly half the birds on earth migrate, spending their summers and winters in different places often thousands of miles apart. Some birds spend most of their lives in the air. Swifts land only to breed and fly non-stop for up to three years, sleeping, drinking, eating and even mating on the wing. Other birds seem to fly just for fun. Fulmars clearly enjoy banking and turning, with their wings stiff and outstretched, as perilously close to the ocean waves as they dare.*

*Many animals can fly, but birds are the real masters of the air. They can soar, glide, hover, twist and turn, dive and perform aerobatics. Penguins can even 'fly' underwater, while peregrine falcons can move so fast during their aerial dives that they reach speeds of up to 150 miles (240 km) per hour.*

*Even the daily routine acts of take-off, level flight, turning, accelerating, slowing down and landing are no less remarkable. Birds are perfectly adapted for every aspect of flight. Their hearts are large, their lungs powerful and their bones light and strong. Their body feathers provide streamlining, while their tail feathers help with steering and balance. Even their flexible wings are curved slightly from front to back, producing an aerofoil profile which literally pulls them upwards as they flap through the air.*

*The precise shape of the wings varies according to the kind of flying the birds need to do. Woodpeckers have short, rounded wings for manoeuvrability in their tangled woodland homes,*

**MARTIAL EAGLE**
*(Polemaetus bellicosus)*

while albatrosses have long, thin wings for gliding over the southern seas.

Flying uses up a great deal of energy. Take-off is the most demanding moment of all and, the heavier the bird, the more difficult this becomes. Penguins need so much fat to survive in the cold that, given suitable wings, they would still be much too heavy to fly. Even a large vulture, when full of food, has to run along the ground to gain sufficient speed to become airborne.

No one yet knows how a fossil bird found in Argentina, called Argentavis magnificens, ever managed to get airborne. It weighed more than a large rhea and had a wingspan of about 23 ft (7 m). Swans, pelicans, great bustards and marabou storks weighing up to about 30 lb (14 kg) are among the largest flying birds today.

**JAY**
*(Garrulus glandarius)*

The energy costs of flying are so high that birds seem to abandon flight whenever they get the chance. The first to do this was an extraordinary, man-sized diver called Hesperornis, which evolved from its flying ancestors 120 million years ago. Many more birds have since lost the ability to fly, among them kiwis, kakapos, cassowaries, ostriches, emus and Galapagos cormorants.

Flight probably evolved as a means of escape from hungry dinosaurs and, although the dinosaurs have gone, reverting to flightlessness is still risky if there are predators around.

Most flightless birds live on remote islands where they evolved in safe isolation from predators – until people arrived with all their rats, cats, dogs and other predatory animals. Unable to cope with the onslaught, many of these special birds are now threatened with extinction or have already disappeared. The classic example is the dodo, which became extinct on its island home of Mauritius just over 300 years ago. Would it have survived if it had retained its ability to fly?

**BLACK-HEADED GULL**
*(Larus ridibundus)* RIGHT

## MAGNIFICENT FRIGATEBIRD
### *(Fregata magnificens)*

RIGHT: **M**agnificent frigatebirds have the greatest wing area, relative to body size, of any bird. They are spectacular in flight, combining the speed and agility of a falcon with the soaring and gliding powers of a vulture. The birds are unable to settle on the sea because their feathers are not waterproof, and swoop down to catch fish or squid swimming near the surface. Unmistakable in flight, they have deeply forked tails and long, angular, pointed wings, with a span of up to 8 ft (2.4 m). The males have bright-red throat pouches which they inflate to attract the females. Magnificent frigatebirds live mainly on tropical coasts and islands of the Atlantic and Pacific Oceans.

. . . . . . . . . . . . . . . . . . . .

## CHILEAN FLAMINGO
### *(Phoenicopterus ruber chilensis)*

RIGHT: **F**lamingos may look unreal and rather grotesque on the ground, but a flock of them in the air is a breathtaking sight. They have impressively long legs and necks, which are essential for feeding in deep water, but which cause enormous problems once the birds have taken off. Their large wings enable them to fly fairly fast but, with their necks outstretched and legs trailing behind, their flying skills are otherwise quite limited. The Chilean flamingo is a South American bird, one of three sub-species of the greater flamingo.

. . . . . . . . . . . . . . . . . . .

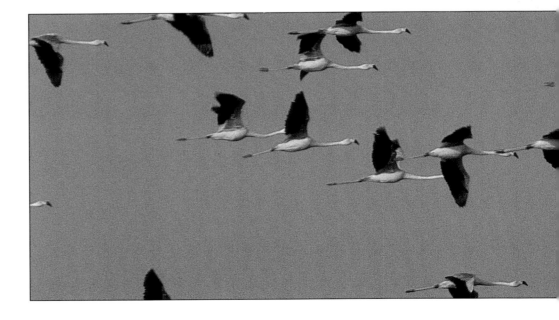

### CANADA GOOSE
### (Branta canadensis)

LEFT: Canada geese are highly gregarious birds outside the breeding season. They gather in noisy and well-organised flocks, and have aggressively maintained pecking orders. When moving at dusk and dawn between their roosts on water and their feeding grounds in open fields, they fly with rather laboured wingbeats.
Yet they are surprisingly strong and powerful birds and are capable of migrating very long distances. Introduced to Europe and New Zealand from North America, they vary in size more than any other bird, the largest being as much as seven times heavier than the smallest. Canada geese flocks often contain a few individuals of other species. This picture shows a mixed flock with white-fronted geese *(Anser albifrons)*, so-called because of their conspicuous, broad white foreheads.

....................

### CAPE GANNET
*(Sula capensis)*

Cape gannets breed in noisy colonies on offshore islands in southern Africa. Landing among the crowded nest sites without dropping on to a neighbouring bird can be rather tricky; an arriving gannet therefore opens its tail wide and beats its wings furiously to slow its descent. Gannets have a distinctive method of flying, with alternate periods of flapping and gliding. They usually stay within sight of land, rising higher than most other seabirds and often appearing well above the horizon as they patrol the oceans in search of food. They catch fish such as pilchard, mackerel and mullet by folding back their long, pointed wings and plummeting 100 ft (30 m) or more down to the sea. The enlarged strip of naked black skin on the bird's throat is an adaptation for losing heat in the hot weather.

. . . . . . . . . . . . . . . . . . . .

### FULMAR
#### (Fulmarus glacialis)

ABOVE: **F**ulmars have extraordinary powers of flight. With their feet tucked into their feathers to assist streamlining, they alternately flap and glide on stiff wings, sweeping low across the water. They are widespread throughout the Arctic, Atlantic and North Pacific, and have recently shown a remarkable increase in both range and numbers, having learnt to supplement their natural diet of crustaceans and small fish with new, man-made sources of food. At the height of the whaling industry, fulmars scavenged on whale carcasses; nowadays, they gather in enormous numbers around trawlers, gorging themselves on the steady flow of fish offal provided by the crews as they gut their catches. They are notorious for spitting an oil from their stomachs as a form of defence; this oil smells awful and is almost impossible to get out of clothing. Although fulmars look rather like gulls, they are, in fact, relatives of the petrels and shearwaters.

. . . . . . . . . . . . . . . . . . .

### WHITE TERN
#### (Gygis alba)

CENTRE LEFT: **T**he white tern is particularly delicate and graceful for a seabird. It is the only tern with an all-white plumage and has beautiful, translucent wings. These may provide effective camouflage against the bright sky before the bird swoops down to catch fish near the surface of the sea. The white tern is a widespread bird which nests on tropical islands as far apart as the Seychelles, Ascension and Easter Island and spends the remainder of the year at sea. It is also known as the white noddy, love tern or fairy tern, although the true fairy tern (Sterna nereis) is a different species altogether with a distinctive black cap.

. . . . . . . . . . . . . . . . . . .

### ARCTIC TERN
#### (Sterna paradisaea)

BOTTOM LEFT: **T**he Arctic tern is an elegant but formidable bird. It defends its eggs and chicks by aggressively dive-bombing intruders, regularly striking hard and sometimes even drawing blood; entering a tern colony can be an unnerving experience. The bird is well known as the greatest traveller in the animal kingdom. It breeds around the shores of the Arctic Ocean and in the northern Atlantic and Pacific, and then migrates to the other side of the world to spend the remainder of the year in the Antarctic. A single tern travels up to 25,000 miles (40,000 km) a year on migration alone – and more during its summer and winter stopovers. In a lifetime of 25 years, this is equivalent to a return trip to the Moon.

. . . . . . . . . . . . . . . . . . .

### SNOW PETREL
#### (Pagodroma nivea)

RIGHT: **T**he snow petrel lives further south than almost any other animal in the world. It nests along the shores of Antarctica and neighbouring islands, sometimes as far as 150 miles (250 km) inland. From a distance, or in poor light, it often appears pale grey in colour, although it is actually pure white. It frequently changes direction in flight, looking rather like a bat as it hovers, glides and flutters with shallow beats of its long, slender wings, searching for krill and other crustaceans between the icefloes and icebergs.

. . . . . . . . . . . . . . . . . . .

### CATTLE EGRET
### (Bubulcus ibis)

LEFT: **C**attle egrets usually assemble near water before going to roost. However, unlike most other egrets, they prefer to forage in fields and meadows, and their name comes from their habit of feeding near cattle. Perched on the animals' backs, or moving fearlessly around their feet, the egrets dive on insects that have been stirred up or dislodged. In return, they provide an early-warning system to the cattle by taking flight at the first hint of danger. They also feed around wild herbivores – zebras, wildebeest and even elephants – as they did for thousands of years before people replaced game animals with cattle. Cattle egrets are exceptionally successful birds: in the past 40 years, they have colonised both North America and Australia unaided and now occur virtually worldwide.

. . . . . . . . . . . . . . . . . . .

### GREAT WHITE EGRET
### (Egretta alba)

ABOVE: **T**he great white egret is one of the largest and most widespread members of the heron family. There has been much confusion over its name in the past, with American egret, common egret, large egret, white egret and great white egret all commonly used in various parts of the world. With its long neck tucked in and legs trailing behind, it is capable of flying very long distances, although its wingbeat is rather slow. Only non-breeding and immature birds have yellow bills which, as the breeding season approaches, gradually turn black.

. . . . . . . . . . . . . . . . . . .

### MALLARD
#### (Anas platyrhynchos)

ABOVE: **T**he mallard can take off easily from either water or land, rising almost vertically if it is leaving a confined space. The ancestor of most domestic breeds of duck, it is widespread throughout much of the northern hemisphere and a familiar sight in almost any kind of waterside habitat, including city parks. The male is unmistakable, with his striking, bottle-green head and chocolate-brown breast. Surprisingly, it is the comparatively rather drab, mottled-brown female that quacks. The male makes weaker, more highly pitched, whistling and grunting sounds.

.....................

### MUTE SWAN
#### (Cygnus olor)

RIGHT: **T**he long-necked and short-legged mute swan is not a very mobile bird on land and has to make a laborious pattering run along the water in order to get airborne. Once in the air, however, its flight is fast and smooth, and its slow, steady, powerful wingbeats create an uncanny throbbing sound that carries for miles. A familiar bird of waterways in both town and country, the mute swan is the commonest swan in Europe, although in recent years it has shown a serious decline in some areas caused mainly by poisoning from anglers' discarded lead weights. It also occurs in parts of Asia, and has been introduced into North America, South Africa, Australia and New Zealand.

.....................

### BLUE CRANE
*(Anthropoides paradisea)*

LEFT: **T**he blue crane normally flies with its legs trailing out behind it. When flying in cold weather, however, it prefers to keep its feet warm by tucking them under its breast feathers. One of the most beautiful and graceful of all African birds, it is a very strong flier. It soars well, often calling its distinctive and very loud, guttural, rattling croak from great heights. The blue crane is short-billed compared with many other cranes, and eats a wide range of food, including grass seeds, shoots and small animals such as frogs, insects and fish.

. . . . . . . . . . . . . . . . . . . . .

### MARABOU STORK
*(Leptoptilos crumeniferus)*

ABOVE: **T**he marabou stork is so huge that its leg and toe bones are hollow to keep its weight down for flying. Its long, dangling, pink throat sac makes it a rather unattractive bird. This sac is air-filled and connected to the breathing system; it is not used for holding food. Marabou storks spend much of the time standing around doing nothing, but they have voracious appetites and will eat anything from termites to flamingos. They often feed on carrion, mixing with vultures on the African savanna, and thrusting their heads deep inside the body cavities of dead animals.

. . . . . . . . . . . . . . . . . . . .

### STARLING
*(Sturnus vulgaris)*

ABOVE: **As** the sun begins to set, enormous flocks of starlings
gather for their daily flights into towns and cities. From a
distance they look like clouds of smoke – but they give the game
away with their incessant bickering and chattering. Wheeling
and turning with impressive synchronisation, they perform
spectacular massed flights over their favourite roosts before
settling down for the night. Window ledges and rooftops
everywhere are brought alive with their ceaseless activity (and
are covered very quickly with their droppings). Starlings are
widespread birds that occur virtually worldwide.

. . . . . . . . . . . . . . . . . . . .

### STRAW-NECKED IBIS
*(Threskiornis spinicollis)*

LEFT: **A** small party of straw-necked ibises flying in V-formation
to their nightime roost is an unforgettable sight. Alternately
flapping and gliding, and calling their hoarse, drawn-out croaks
and grunts, they are distinctive birds. Their long, thin, down-
curved bills, which are characteristic of all the ibises, show
clearly in silhouette. These ibises are remarkably nomadic,
dispersing widely during droughts in the hope of finding the
unpredictable and intermittently flooded marshes which they
need for breeding. Also known as dryweather birds or
letterbirds, they live in Indonesia and New Guinea and are the
commonest of the three Australian ibises.

. . . . . . . . . . . . . . . . . . . .

# CHAPTER TWO

# AVIAN COMMUNITIES

. . . . . . . . . . . . . . . . . . . .

**CRAB PLOVER**
*(Dromas ardeola)*

SOME BIRDS PREFER *their own company, ignoring or avoiding others of their kind for most of the year. But there are many which are more sociable and prefer to live in anything from small groups to communities of thousands or even hundreds of thousands. 'Togetherness' can be either a weakness or a virtue. It depends largely upon the kind of food a bird eats. Hawks rely on stealth, speed and skill to catch their prey and would probably catch very little if they hunted in ungainly and conspicuous flocks. But pelicans are more successful when they organise themselves into co-operative 'fishing schools' because a fish swimming away from one bird is likely to swim straight towards another.*

*Safety in numbers is also an important consideration. When 'birds of a feather flock together' they are more likely to spot impending danger than would one bird on its own. And the bigger the flock, the more time each bird can devote to feeding or preening rather than to keeping watch.*

*Many birds find the company of others useful only at certain times of the year. Some flock during the winter but split up at the beginning of the breeding season, others do the same thing in reverse.*

**OSTRICH**
*(Struthio camelus)*

*Whether the flock is temporary or permanent, the birds will often organise themselves into a fairly rigid pecking order. This is a useful way of resolving disputes without constantly fighting. Each*

**IMPERIAL SHAG**
*(Phalacrocorax atriceps)*

bird knows its position in the hierarchy and, when there is competition for something especially desirable, it is aware that it takes priority over some members of the group and must give way to others.

In one of the most extraordinary of all avian communities, male black grouse organise themselves into very tight hierarchies when they gather at their communal display grounds. Dominant males maintain the prime locations near the centre, where they are most likely to attract females, and each defends its own small patch of land against potential rivals.

Like the black grouse, and like many people, even the most sociable birds often prefer to retain their own 'personal space'. Starlings perched on a telegraph wire usually sit very evenly spaced, each a few inches away from its neighbours. But there are many exceptions. Parrots, emperor penguins, wrens and a variety of other birds depend upon, or enjoy, each other's company so much that they prefer to sit cheek-by-jowl in tight huddles.

**LESSER NODDY**
(*Anous tenuirostris*)

When living in such close proximity, it is impossible to ignore what other members of a flock are doing. Birds tend to copy each other – when one starts to preen, or to feed, the others will often join in. If one suddenly takes to the air, it is likely that the others will rapidly follow suit.

**BRUNNICH'S GUILLEMOT**
(*Uria lomvia*)

## AUSTRALIAN GANNET
### (Sula serrator)

ABOVE: The birds in this picture were photographed at one of the few mainland gannet colonies anywhere in the world, at Muriwai, near Auckland, New Zealand. Most gannets breed on the tops of small islands or rock stacks and form enormous crowded colonies. The Australian species builds a pedestal nest of seaweed, often padded with other vegetation, guano and soft earth, usually just out of pecking range of its neighbours. The young birds are mainly brown, but they have a white dot at the end of each feather which gives them a distinctive mottled appearance. Within a year of leaving the colony, they closely resemble their parents, but they are not identical until they are at least three or four years old.

. . . . . . . . . . . . . . . . . . .

## HEERMANN'S GULL
### (Larus heermanni)

LEFT: These gulls are widespread and common along the coasts of the western United States and north-west Mexico, often occurring in large flocks near their favourite feeding grounds. They spend a considerable amount of time near cormorants and pelicans, sea otters and seals, swooping down to steal their food or to retrieve lost scraps. The largest concentrations of Heermann's gulls occur at their breeding colonies, notably on the island of Raza in the Gulf of California, where several-hundred-thousand pairs gather to nest. Most of the birds in this picture are adults in their distinctive summer plumage; the chocolate-brown birds are one-year-olds.

. . . . . . . . . . . . . . . . . . .

## ADELIE PENGUIN
### (Pygoscelis adeliae)

LEFT: **E**very October, when the southern seas are still frozen, Adelie penguins begin to return to their rookeries around the coasts and islands of the Antarctic. They are unable to fly, and to get to the rookeries must sometimes walk and toboggan, on their bellies, across as much as 60 miles (96 km) of ice. The rookeries are enormous: some exceed one-million birds, which eat an estimated 9,000 tons of krill every day. Adelie penguins are bold and inquisitive birds that are always curious about what their colleagues are up to. If one begins to stroll along a beach or dives into the sea, the others in the group will often be unable to resist the temptation to follow. Their main predators are in the water, and include leopard seals and other seals, killer whales and sharks.

. . . . . . . . . . . . . . . . . . . .

## KING PENGUIN
### (Aptenodytes patagonicus)

ABOVE AND BELOW: **K**ing penguins are very sociable birds. In their sub-Antarctic rookeries, they often huddle together to keep warm during the coldest weather or severe blizzards. They have two main egg-laying seasons, so a single colony always contains a harmonious mixture of adults, chicks and eggs. They do not build nests – and have no territories to defend – so they are relatively peaceful birds. An adult wanders freely around the colony, incubating its single large egg on the top of its feet. The chicks, which are covered in thick, woolly brown down, often form large groups of their own, called creches, where they wait to be fed enormous meals of squid and small fish by their parents. King penguins like to breed on flat ground near the shore, within easy reach of the sea.

. . . . . . . . . . . . . . . . . . . .

## KITTIWAKE
### (Rissa tridactyla)

**K**ittiwakes are more pelagic than most gulls and spend much of
their time wandering far out at sea. They come to land to breed
on steep sea cliffs, forming enormous colonies such as the one in
this picture, on the island of Grimsey in Iceland. Because there
are so many birds that every available ledge has to be used, there
is considerable rivalry between the birds as they stake out their
territories at the beginning of the breeding season. Some of the
ledges are so ridiculously tiny and precarious that the birds must
press themselves awkwardly against the rock to avoid being
blown off, and they have strong claws on their webbed feet for
clinging on to their nests. Thousands more kittiwakes wheel
constantly over the sea around these colonies, filling the air with
their incessant wailing – a familiar call which sounds like 'kitti-
week', as if the birds are repeating their name.

....................

### WHOOPER SWAN
*(Cygnus cygnus)*

On their breeding grounds across much of northern Europe and Asia, whooper swans defend well-spaced territories. At other times of the year they are very sociable birds, congregating in flocks of up to 300. The winter gathering in this picture was photographed at a lake in Japan. New arrivals joining such a flock are usually greeted with much excited calling. Whooper swans are among the noisiest swans in the world, making a variety of evocative trumpeting and honking calls which can be heard over great distances. When in flight, they make the characteristic 'whoop-whoop-whoop' call which gives them their name.

....................

### AMERICAN WHITE PELICAN
*(Pelecanus erythrorhynchos)*

LEFT: American white pelicans can often be seen working in teams, known as 'fishing schools'. They swim in a horseshoe-shape to encircle a shoal of fish and, with immaculate timing, plunge their heads into the water in unison to scoop up the prey. The birds stay together during migration, forming large flocks that travel over land in V-formation, often at considerable heights. Confined to North America, the American white pelican is locally common in breeding colonies of several-hundred pairs, usually nesting on the islands of inland lakes. It is one of seven pelican species found in different parts of the world.

. . . . . . . . . . . . . . . . . . . .

### AUSTRALIAN PELICAN
*(Pelecanus conspicillatus)*

ABOVE: Australian pelicans are sociable birds that prefer the company of others to being alone, and they rest, feed, breed and fly together. When travelling long distances they fly in V-formation or in long lines, spiralling upwards on one thermal updraft and gliding down on outstretched wings to the next. Sometimes known as spectacled pelicans because of the small, featherless rings around their eyes, they are found anywhere in Australia where there is a large body of water and plenty of food. They are also casual visitors to New Guinea, Indonesia and New Zealand. The smaller birds in this picture are silver gulls *(Larus novaehollandiae)*.

. . . . . . . . . . . . . . . . . . . .

### BLACK VULTURE
### *(Coragyps atratus)*

**I**f a vulture, soaring high in the air, spots a carcass, it begins to
circle lower. Neighbouring vultures notice this sudden change in
direction and fly nearer to investigate; their neighbours then
follow suit. Within minutes, vultures are converging on the
carcass from miles around. The first birds to arrive like to spend
some time sitting on a nearby vantage point – such as the cacti in
this picture – before finally dropping on to their meal. Black
vultures are not particularly good at spotting carrion and often
keep a close eye on turkey vultures *(Cathartes aura)*, in case
they find anything. They are fairly common birds in many parts
of the United States and in Central and South America. They eat
mostly carrion, but will also take young or sick animals and often
invade towns and villages to feed on garbage.

. . . . . . . . . . . . . . . . . . .

### SCARLET MACAW
#### (Ara macao)
### RED AND GREEN MACAW
#### (Ara chloroptera)

ABOVE: Macaws are large, long-tailed members of the parrot family, well-known for their apparent intelligence and harsh, screaming calls. Sadly, they are familiar to most people as caged birds. Parrots have been kept as pets for nearly 2,500 years and today a huge range of species is kept in captivity. Macaws are particularly popular because of their striking colours and long lives and, as a consequence, are trapped in large numbers in their native Central and South America. The mixed flock of birds in this picture is congregating at a natural salt-lick. The two species can be distinguished by their 'median wing coverts', or shoulders, which are bright yellow on the scarlet macaws and green on the red and green macaws.

. . . . . . . . . . . . . . . . . . . .

### SNOW GOOSE
#### (Anser caerulescens)

RIGHT: This beautiful goose of the Arctic occurs in two different colour forms. Both of these belong to the same species but one is totally white with black wingtips, while the other is dark grey with a white head and neck.

There is also a variety of intermediates between these so-called 'white' and 'blue' phases. Snow geese are gregarious birds throughout the year, breeding in closely packed colonies on the Arctic tundra. Within a flock – which may number tens of thousands of birds – small family parties tend to stay together. In flight the geese call almost continuously and, from a distance, sound rather like a pack of small yapping dogs.

. . . . . . . . . . . . . . . . . . . .

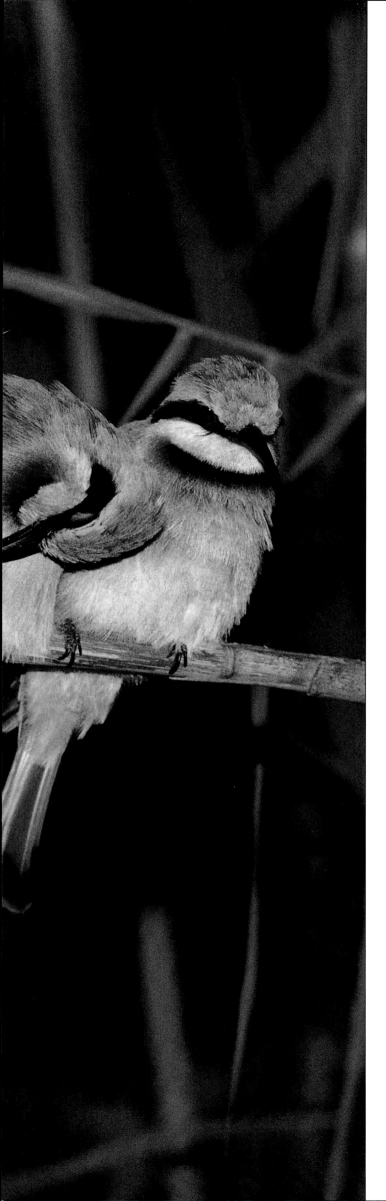

**LITTLE BEE-EATER**
*(Merops pusillus)*

LEFT: There are 24 different species of bee-eater, all brightly coloured and all with distinctive black eye-stripes. Little bee-eaters are the smallest members of the family and are common birds in Africa south of the Sahara. They usually spend the daytime alone, quietly perched on small bushes or grass stems near the ground, keeping watch for bees and other insects to eat. The birds sometimes live in pairs or, more rarely, in small family groups. However, they appear to enjoy more company at nightime and often roost together, perched on branches in tightly bunched rows.

. . . . . . . . . . . . . . . . . . .

**SCALED DOVE**
*(Columbina squammata)*

ABOVE: The body feathers of scaled doves each have a conspicuous black edge, making the birds look as if they are covered in reptilian-like scales. This gives them their name in English, although in their native South America most of the local Spanish names refer to the strange, rattling sound that their wings make as they fly. Scaled doves occur naturally in open woods and scrubland, where they live in pairs or in small flocks. However, they show little fear of humans and often venture into suburban areas. This group of roosting birds was photographed in the Pantanal, Brazil.

. . . . . . . . . . . . . . . . . . .

### LITTLE CORELLA
*(Cacatua sanguinea)*

From a distance, the little corella appears to be snow white in colour. However, its other name – the blood-stained cockatoo – is more indicative of its true appearance. There is a pink stain between its bill and eyes, and when the bird preens or the wind ruffles its coat, rich-pink underfeathers can be seen all over its head and throat. Unlike most cockatoos, the little corella's head is almost crestless. However, in keeping with family tradition, it does like to live with others of its kind. This flock of noisy birds was photographed at a cattle station in Queensland, Australia.

.....................

# CHAPTER THREE

# BIRDS AT REST

. . . . . . . . . . . . . . . . . . . .

**ORANGE-BREASTED
SUNBIRD**
*(Nectarinia violacea)*

LIKE ALL ANIMALS, *birds need to rest. They sleep or doze in an amusing variety of positions – while lying down, standing on both legs, balancing on one leg, sitting on water, squashed inside rock crevices, or even while on the wing. Ostriches sleep with their necks outstretched and resting on the ground.*

*Some birds sleep huddled together in enormous colonies, where they are able to keep warm and conserve energy. One huge roost of red-billed queleas in Sudan was estimated to contain more than 30-million birds. Rooks have a special hierarchy in their roosts, in which the older and more experienced adults are allowed the warmest locations near the centre, away from cold draughts and winds. Other birds prefer to sleep alone. A tawny owl selects a comfortable branch hidden by thick foliage where it can spend the day fast asleep.*

*Certain owls, nightjars and other nocturnal species are often asleep during the day, but most birds sleep at night. It really depends on their feeding habits. Waders, for example, feed when the tide is out, whether it is day or night. But when*

**BLACK-NECKED GREBE**
*(Podiceps nigricollis)*

**BROWN KIWI**
*(Apteryx australis)*

birds do settle down they often hide themselves in the most unlikely places – on floating rafts, inside street lamps, on windowsills, in greenhouses and even on sewage-farm sprinklers. Their main concern is to shelter from the elements and to conceal themselves from predators. Some birds rely more on camouflage, hoping they will be overlooked if they keep still and blend in with their surroundings.

There are birds that go for long periods with hardly any sleep at all, just snatching a few seconds rest whenever they can. In contrast, the North American poorwill nightjar hibernates for up to five months during the worst winter weather.

In particularly cold weather, many birds save energy by sitting still for long periods during the day. As darkness falls, pigeons, finches and other seed-eating birds collect food in their crops and carry it to their roosts. Comfortably settled in, they digest their meals slowly to reduce the length of the long winter night's fast.

Some birds have an enforced period of rest when they moult. Usually, when they renew their worn-out flight feathers these are lost gradually over a period of many weeks so that flight itself, although impaired, is still possible. But the larger auks and some ducks lose all their flight feathers at once and, for a period, are completely flightless.

**EGYPTIAN GOOSE**
*(Alopochen aegyptiacus)*

Finally, there are the birds that do a certain amount of idle loafing. Their apparent inactivity may be deceptive: birds of prey and fly-catchers could be alert and looking for prey. But there are birds that, on occasion, seem to sit around and watch the world go by, as if they were day-dreaming and had nothing better to do.

**BLUE-CROWNED MOTMOT**
*(Momotus momota)*

### LITTLE AUK
### *(Alle alle)*

ABOVE: **A**lthough hardly bigger than a
starling, the little auk, or dovekie, is a
surprisingly tough little bird. It spends the
winter far out at sea, rarely coming within
sight of land, and breeds among snow-covered
boulder screes in the high Arctic. With some
of the larger colonies numbering more than a
million birds, a visit to a little auk colony can
be a memorable experience. The air is alive
with their shrill chattering and, at a distance,
small flocks of the birds look like swarms of
mosquitos, as they wheel and turn on whirring
wings. They lay their eggs in gaps between the
boulders, and every piece of rock seems to
have an auk perched on it. The bird in this
picture was photographed outside its
nest in Spitsbergen.

. . . . . . . . . . . . . . . . . . . .

### RED-FAN PARROT
### *(Deroptyus accipitrinus)*

RIGHT: **S**trange, wailing cries can sometimes
be heard in the tropical rain forests of
northern South America. These are made by
red-fan parrots, which feed on palm fruits in
the forest canopy. Living either alone or in
small flocks, they are difficult birds to see,
except on their occasional forays to cultivated
land, where they feed on guava and other fruit
crops. Otherwise known as hawk-headed
parrots, they have a broad band of crimson
and blue feathers on the nape, which usually
lies flat but can be erected to form a beautiful,
fan-shaped crest. Red-fan parrots are in great
demand as cage birds and, sadly, the high
prices that they fetch in upper Amazonia and
other places are encouraging the capture of
the birds in the wild.

. . . . . . . . . . . . . . . . . . . .

## SADDLE-BILLED STORK
### (Ephippiorhynchus senegalensis)

LEFT: The saddlebill is the largest stork in Africa. A huge bird, it is 5 ft (1.5 m) tall and has a wingspan of nearly 9 ft (2.7 m). Despite its size, it is shy and rather nervous, preferring to live either alone or in pairs, rather than in large gatherings. It is an adept hunter, which stalks its prey like a heron by walking slowly in shallow water with its head down, looking for fish, frogs and other small animals. Its bill darts out and the unsuspecting creatures are sometimes tossed in the air before being recaptured and swallowed.

. . . . . . . . . . . . . . . . . . . .

## YELLOW-BILLED STORK
### (Ibis ibis)

RIGHT: The yellow-billed stork spends a great deal of its time quietly doing nothing. A common bird in many parts of Africa, it stands around for much of the day, usually either in a small party of its own species or with a mixed group of spoonbills, herons and other large wading birds. During the night, it sleeps in communal roosts located in trees or on sandbanks. Even when hunting, this stork is slow and purposeful. It walks around in a marsh, or in the shallows of a river, casually stirring up the mud with its feet, and holding its bill underwater and slightly open. It can feel any fish, frogs, insects or other small animals which are disturbed by the stirring and grab them before they have a chance to escape.

. . . . . . . . . . . . . . . . . . . .

### CARDINAL
#### *(Cardinalis cardinalis)*

ABOVE: **C**ardinals are common birds throughout much of North and Central America, where they live along woodland edges and in hedgerows, parks and suburban gardens. They are popular birds and, because so many people feed them during the winter, they have rapidly expanded their range in recent years. This picture shows a male, which is an unmistakable and striking bright-red colour; the females are a duller olive-brown. Both sexes are enthusiastic songsters, singing their loud and varied whistles all year round.

. . . . . . . . . . . . . . . . . . . .

### CINNAMON-CHESTED BEE-EATER
#### *(Merops oreobates)*

LEFT: **B**ee-eaters sometimes sit on branches to relax and sunbathe. However, their apparent inactivity can be deceptive. They use similar perches as vantage points for hunting and may be scanning the air for passing bees. The African cinnamon-chested bee-eater chooses a branch high above the ground and, as it sits there, it is fully alert. It turns its head from side to side until it spots a likely meal, then darts out and, with astonishing speed and precision, seizes its prey in its long, slightly downward-curving beak. The bee-eater then glides back to its perch, and removes the poison sacs and sting before swallowing the bee whole. It also eats wasps, hornets and other flying insects. These juvenile birds have not yet developed the characteristic, cinnamon-coloured chests of their parents.

. . . . . . . . . . . . . . . . . . . .

## OYSTERCATCHER
### *(Haematopus ostralegus)*

These brash and distinctive birds are a
familiar sight on estuaries and rocky shores in
many parts of Europe, Asia and North Africa.
Some of their winter gatherings are huge, with
tens of thousands of birds concentrating on
favoured high-tide roosts. They are noisy
birds and even a lone oystercatcher will make
its presence known with a continuous, sharp
'kleep-kleep' call. Although all oystercatchers
have long, orange-red bills, there are, in fact,
two varieties of bill. One of these has a blunt
tip for *hammering* open bivalve molluscs such
as mussels and cockles; the other has a
chisel-shaped tip for *prizing* them open, or for
stabbing the muscles that hold the two halves
of the shells together. Young birds learn from
their parents to follow either one method of
obtaining their food or the other.

. . . . . . . . . . . . . . . . . . . .

### YELLOW-BILLED OXPECKER
*(Buphagus africanus)*

Oxpeckers spend much of their time
perched on the backs of cattle and big-game
animals, clinging to their hides with strong,
sharp claws, and propping themselves up with
their stiff tail feathers. These members of the
starling family feed on the blood-gorged ticks
which live on many of the animals inhabiting
their dry, African-savanna home. Oxpeckers
are allowed to clamber all over their hosts —
even to probe inside their ears and nostrils. In
return, they rid the animals of unwelcome
parasites and provide an early-warning system
when danger threatens. Yellow-billed
oxpeckers are not particularly common birds.
Their numbers have declined with recent
reductions in game numbers and because of
cattle dipping, which reduces the
number of ticks.

. . . . . . . . . . . . . . . . . . .

## EUROPEAN EAGLE OWL
### (Bubo bubo)

ABOVE LEFT: This largest and most powerful of all the owls grows up to 28 in (71 cm) in length and has a wingspan of more than 5 ft (1.5 m). An opportunist, it will eat almost anything it can overcome – other owls included – and has been known to hunt animals as large as roe deer. Its normal prey, however, consists of rats and other small mammals. The 'ear tufts' on this owl's head have no connection with its hearing: they are merely elongated head feathers used for camouflage and to communicate moods or intentions to other owls.

. . . . . . . . . . . . . . . . . . .

## GREAT GREY OWL
### (Strix nebulosa)

OPPOSITE: Great grey owls are absurdly bold birds. They will stare back almost disdainfully at a person standing only a few yards away. On other occasions, they seem to find people so fascinating that they cannot resist a closer look, and it is not unusual for them to sit on the same perch for several hours, watching woodcutters at work in a forest. But they often do not tolerate intruders near their nests and will defend their young aggressively. As a result of this, several people have lost their eyes to the owls, while others have been knocked to the ground. Despite their large size and obvious strength, great grey owls feed almost entirely on voles and shrews. They have a vast circumpolar range throughout the northern coniferous forests of America, Europe and Asia.

. . . . . . . . . . . . . . . . . . .

## BURROWING OWL
### (Athene cunicularia)

ABOVE AND RIGHT: Burrowing owls spend a great deal of time on the ground, which is why their legs are noticeably longer than those of most other owls. As their name suggests, they are capable of digging their own underground burrows for both roosting and nesting. However, they usually prefer to adapt the abandoned burrows of prairie dogs, and if they come across a complex of these ready-made homes, they move in together to form a small colony. They employ a special alarm call, which sounds uncannily like a rattlesnake, to deter intruders from entering the burrows when they are inside. Burrowing owls live in open country such as rough grassland and golf courses, where they hunt beetles, rodents, birds, reptiles and other small animals. During the daytime, they can often be seen standing around looking rather bored near their burrow entrances.

. . . . . . . . . . . . . . . . . . .

### GALAPAGOS HAWK
#### (Buteo galapagoensis)

Grazing giant tortoises are often used as convenient perches by
hawks in the Galapagos Islands. Found nowhere else in the
world, Galapagos hawks are the only diurnal raptors in the area.
Like many other Galapagos animals, they have no fear of people
and the young, in particular, have an unquenchable curiosity.
They are adaptable birds and will eat almost anything, from
grasshoppers and caterpillars to marine iguanas and carrion.
Their remarkable tameness made them easy targets for the early
settlers, who believed – wrongly – that the hawks were preying
on their livestock. More recently, large numbers were killed for
preying on chickens and they have now disappeared from many
of the islands on which they once lived.

. . . . . . . . . . . . . . . . . . . .

**BLACK-CROWNED NIGHT HERON**
*(Nycticorax nycticorax)*

ABOVE: **A**s dusk begins to fall, black-crowned night herons leave the trees, bushes and dense waterside vegetation where they have been dozing quietly all day, and start hunting. Perched just above the water, they remain motionless for long periods, looking for fish, frogs, crabs and other aquatic animals. They sometimes also eat small mammals and birds, and will steal the eggs and young of other herons at their nesting colonies. Black-crowned night herons are the most cosmopolitan members of the heron family, living in a wide range of wetland habitats almost worldwide. The bird in this picture is sharing its hunting perch with a group of freshwater turtles *(Podocnemys vogli)*.

. . . . . . . . . . . . . . . . . . . .

**AMERICAN BITTERN**
*(Botaurus lentiginosus)*

RIGHT: **T**he American bittern is a fairly common, but elusive, bird. It skulks in dense marsh reedbeds and is so well camouflaged that it blends in perfectly with its surroundings. When alarmed, it freezes, remaining motionless in a reed-like pose with its long bill pointing skyward, and disappearing almost completely. American bitterns are also sometimes known as 'thunder-pumpers' because of their strange cry – a pumping sound like 'oonk-a-stunk' – which is always a conclusive sign of their presence. They feed on fish, crabs, frogs and other small animals, moving slowly through the reeds ready to jab at their prey with lightning speed.

. . . . . . . . . . . . . . . . . . . .

### CROWNED CRANE
### *(Balearica pavonina)*

ABOVE: The crowned crane is one of the oldest members of the crane family, having been around for as long as 50 million years. It is an elegant bird, named after the magnificent crest of straw-coloured plumes on its head. Its striking appearance and relative tameness have made it a popular pet with some people. Despite this, it is still fairly common in many parts of Africa, where it frequents marshes, grasslands and open plains. It spends much of the day hunting for frogs, reptiles and insects but, unlike most other members of the family, prefers to roost in trees.

. . . . . . . . . . . . . . . . . . . .

### BLUE-WINGED TEAL
### *(Anas discors)*

LEFT: Blue-winged teals are shy and wary birds that often prefer to rest on branches protruding from the water, rather than to risk coming on to land. Fairly common and widespread, they breed in North America, from southern Canada to Mexico, and winter as far south as northern Chile and northern Argentina. They prefer open country, where they live in small flocks on marshes, ponds and lakes, feeding by dabbling on the surface of the water or by up-ending just beneath it. Both sexes have chalky-blue 'shoulders', although the male is most conspicuous because he has a prominent white crescent in front of each eye.

. . . . . . . . . . . . . . . . . . . .

### KESTREL
#### (Falco tinnunculus)

ABOVE: **K**estrels are cautiously tolerant of people and, in recent years, have found a niche for themselves along roadside verges. Like other falcons, they sometimes use speed with an element of surprise to capture small birds. More often, however, they can be seen perched on overhead wires, telegraph poles or even road bridges, scanning the ground for tell-tale movements in the grass below. Their visual acuity is several times better than our own, and they can spot small-prey animals such as voles, beetles or earthworms from a considerable height. When hunting, they hover 100 ft (30 m) or more above the ground. They are also known as wind-hovers and literally hang motionless in the wind before dropping gradually on to their prey. Kestrels are familiar birds in much of Europe, Africa and Asia.

. . . . . . . . . . . . . . . . . . .

### AFRICAN FISH EAGLE
#### (Haliaeetus vocifer)

RIGHT: **T**here are few sounds more evocative than the loud, clear call of an African fish eagle. The bird throws its head back and emits a high-pitched laugh that carries for miles; for many people, this sound characterises the spirit of wild Africa. Fish eagles live near large rivers and lakes and, although they will take a variety of food, including frogs, waterbirds and even monkeys, as their names suggests, they feed mainly on fish. These are caught with their massive, sharp-taloned feet and then taken back to a favourite perch to be eaten. The birds may fish for as little as two hours a week and prefer to spend their time – sometimes most of the day – perched on dead trees near the water's edge. The eagle in this picture spent almost every day for weeks on the same perch in the Okavango Delta, Botswana.

. . . . . . . . . . . . . . . . . . .

### KEA
#### *(Nestor notabilis)*

LEFT: **K**eas are bold, inquisitive and playful birds that love places with people, where they can get up to mischief: they like to slide down roofs, and use their beautiful, long, curved upper bills to untie shoelaces, let air out of car tyres or rip up windscreen wipers. In fact, they are really mountain parrots, living mainly in valley forests and above the treeline to about 7,000 ft (2,100 m). They feed on leaves, buds, fruits and insects, and will even eat carrion. Keas sometimes feed on dead sheep, and it is thought that rogue birds will occasionally peck a sheep to death if they are really hungry. However, their reputation as inveterate sheep killers is undeserved and more than 150,000 have been destroyed by farmers since the beginning of the century. Today, there are about 5,000 keas left, all of which live on South Island, New Zealand, where they are protected by law.

.....................

### HIMALAYAN GRIFFON VULTURE
#### *(Gyps himalayensis)*

RIGHT: **F**or some strange reason, the Himalayan griffon vulture has 14 tail feathers – two more than most other birds. It is a huge vulture, measuring up to 4 ft (1.25 m) in length and, as its name suggests, it lives in the high mountains of the Himalayas, where it has been known to occur in areas up to 24,000 ft (7,440 m) above sea level. Unlike most other vultures, its head and neck are not completely bare but are covered with a fluffy layer of down. This species is very aggressive, and feeds on carrion of all kinds, including dead goats, yaks and even people. The bird in this picture is a juvenile. The ruff of long feathers around its neck is typical of the griffon family.

.....................

# CHAPTER FOUR

# PREENING AND BATHING

**CAPE WHITE-EYE**
*(Zosterops pallidus)*

**F**EATHERS RECEIVE *a constant battering in daily use and need regular care and attention. They get dirty, ruffled, wet and infested with feather lice, fleas and other parasites. Since a bird's survival can depend on the condition of its feathers, keeping them clean is an essential and time-consuming part of its life.*

*Parasites living on the warm, dark skin beneath feathers can be very difficult to remove, but many birds have invented ingenious methods of dealing with them. Hornbills patiently pick off lodgers with their beaks. Jays, jackdaws and starlings encourage ants to crawl all over their bodies — or hold the unfortunate creatures in their beaks and stroke them over their feathers. The irritated ants eject formic acid that acts as a form of insecticide and kills the birds' unwanted guests. House sparrows enjoy dust-bathing, wriggling down into their own little wallow pits and rubbing their heads or throwing the dry sand or earth into their body feathers. The fine particles are forced through the feathers, and scour away any parasites or pieces of dirt hidden in the plumage.*

*Worn feathers are replaced at frequent intervals, but in between moults birds need to keep their plumage supple and water-repellent. Many of them produce a special secretion in an oil gland located near the base of the tail. Reaching over backwards and twisting their tails sideways, they collect the oil in their beaks and carefully anoint each of their feathers*

**BALD EAGLE**
*(Haliaeetus leucocephalus)*

*individually. Herons, parrots, toucans and bowerbirds lack this gland but instead condition their plumage with a fine powder produced by the fraying tips of special powder-down feathers.*

**GREENFINCH**
*(Carduelis chloris)*

*All birds carefully put disarranged feathers back into place, or comb bedraggled ones. They take individual feathers in their beaks and gently fasten the hooks and catches, known as barbs and barbules, which hold them together like a zip. They have particularly flexible necks, with many more vertebrae than in mammals, enabling them to preen almost everywhere except their heads and beaks. Sometimes they use their feet to preen the parts that otherwise cannot be reached.*

*Bathing in water is another way of keeping clean. Birds bathe energetically, but they have to be careful not to soak their plumage. A total drenching would damage the water-proofing of the feathers and, in waterbirds, can dangerously reduce their buoyancy. What appears to be a haphazard splashing is therefore very carefully controlled. Once the feathers have been dampened enough to wash away all the dirt, the water is squeezed out and the bird begins to dry itself.*

*The hot rays of the sun are excellent for drying. A wet African darter will simply stand on a branch with its wings outstretched and pointing towards the sky. The warmth also helps to iron out any twists in the feathers and may even stimulate the flow of preen oil. It is a good excuse for a little sun-bathing — which birds often use to indulge themselves.*

**SUNBITTERN**
*(Eurypyga helias)*

**EUROPEAN WHITE PELICAN**
*(Pelecanus onocrotalus)*

### YELLOW-HEADED AMAZON PARROT
#### (Amazona ochrocephala)

Some birds prefer to take a shower rather than to sit in a bath.
These yellow-headed Amazon parrots are literally showering in
the rain. With their wings held out and feathers erect, they are
exposing as much surface area to the rain as they can without
getting totally drenched. Too much water may damage the
feathers but too little will fail to dislodge all the dirt – so the rain-
bathing is always carefully controlled. The shower over, they
shake their bodies and whirr their wings to rid the plumage of
excess water, then preen their feathers as a final measure to
ensure that they stay in an airworthy condition. Yellow-headed
Amazon parrots are found over much of Central and northern
South America, but are declining in number. They suffer from
forest destruction and, because they have a reputation as good
talkers and mimics, are collected for the cage-bird trade.

. . . . . . . . . . . . . . . . . . . .

## DARTER
### *(Anhinga melanogaster)*

ABOVE: **U**nlike most waterbirds, which keep afloat with the help of air trapped between their waterproof feathers, darters flatten their feathers to expel any trapped air, and this enables them to swim underwater with relative ease. Unfortunately, they get soaking wet in the process and, on leaving the water, have to stand with their wings spread out to allow the feathers to dry. Darters are frequently known as snake-birds – and can indeed be mistaken for snakes in the water – because they often swim partly submerged with only their heads and long, thin, S-shaped necks above the surface. There are four species: the one in the picture is found in many parts of Africa, Asia and Australia.

. . . . . . . . . . . . . . . . . . . .

## BLUE AND YELLOW MACAW
### *(Ara ararauna)*

RIGHT: **P**reening can help to keep the peace between birds in conflict. A submissive bird may present its head for preening to indicate to an opponent that it has decided to surrender. But 'social preening', as it is called, is equally important for removing parasites that would otherwise be out of reach. This is why birds that preen one another usually concentrate on the head region, carefully adjusting position to ensure that all the inaccessible feathers are worked over properly. The blue and yellow macaw is 33 in (84 cm) long – among the largest of all the parrots – and is found in the rain forests and savannas of parts of Central and South America.

. . . . . . . . . . . . . . . . . . . .

### YELLOW-CROWNED NIGHT HERON
*(Nycticorax violaceus)*

OPPOSITE: **A**s its name suggests, the yellow-crowned night heron generally feeds at night, although in the breeding season it is frequently seen during the day as well. It actually has a buff-white crown, rather than a yellow one, and the black and white patterning on its head makes it a distinctive bird. Found in North, Central and South America, it lives in a variety of habitats near water, preferring wooded swamps and coastal thickets. The bird in this picture was photographed in the Galapagos Islands. It is holding its wings open to soak up the sun, possibly to restore its flight feathers a little before preening.

. . . . . . . . . . . . . . . . . . . .

### RED-NECKED PHALAROPE
*(Phalaropus lobatus)*

BELOW: **R**ed-necked phalaropes are as light as a cork. During storms they get blown all over the place and, as a consequence, they have become known as 'gale birds'. This species is found in many parts of the world, and is very tame: the bird in the photograph continued preening and washing while the photographer sat only 4 ft (1.25 m) away. The birds always seem to be eating. One unusual 'fishing' method which they use is to pirouette in the water. This movement creates a small whirlpool, which stirs insects and other small animals into its centre.

. . . . . . . . . . . . . . . . . . . .

### LILAC-BREASTED ROLLER
*(Coracias caudata)*

ABOVE: **W**hen irradiated with sunlight, the oil secreted by a bird's preening gland produces vitamin D. This is absorbed directly through the skin or swallowed during preening, and it may be an important supplement to the bird's diet. Probably for this reason, some birds – such as the lilac-breasted roller in this picture – seem to enjoy sunbathing. The sun also reduces the bird's food requirements by keeping it warm. Lilac-breasted rollers are inhabitants of the African savanna, where they are often attracted to grass fires, possibly because the smoke stimulates their skins. The name 'roller' originates from their spectacular tumbling courtship displays.

. . . . . . . . . . . . . . . . . . . .

**BAR-HEADED GOOSE**
*(Anser indicus)*

ABOVE: **B**ar-headed geese breed in large colonies by the high-plateau lake shores of Tibet and other parts of central Asia. They winter in the northern half of the Indian sub-continent, which requires a migration at exceptional heights over the Himalayas. The birds are shy and nervous during the winter, and often preen their flight feathers first, working on the others at a more leisurely pace when they are confident that their full powers of flight have been restored. Many bar-headed geese have escaped from captivity and survive in the wild in parts of western Europe and North America.

. . . . . . . . . . . . . . . . . . .

**HERRING GULL**
*(Larus argentatus)*

ABOVE: **B**athing is a regular feature of a herring gull's life. Floating on the water, with a carefully structured ritual it ducks its head under the surface, so that the water can then run down its neck and back; it then shakes its wings to create a fine spray. Herring gulls are the familiar 'seagulls' in many parts of the northern hemisphere. They frequently follow fishing boats and their squealing, wailing and chuckling calls are a feature of many seaside towns. Since learning to scavenge on rubbish tips and to nest on rooftops, they have been increasing in both numbers and range.

. . . . . . . . . . . . . . . . . . .

**WHITE-FACED TREE DUCK**
*(Dendrocygna viduata)*

RIGHT: **B**athing is sometimes contagious. The mere sight of one white-faced tree duck having a wash can be enough to arouse the bathing mood in other members of the flock. Like most aquatic species, these ducks bathe while floating on the water, beating their wings to splash the rest of their bodies. They also spend a great deal of time preening both themselves and one another. Mutual preening plays an important role in the formation and maintenance of pair bonds. White-faced tree ducks are common birds throughout much of Africa, Central America and tropical South America. Despite their name, they nest on the ground and rarely perch in trees. They are also known, somewhat more appropriately, as whistling ducks because of their loud, clear 'vee-swee-sweeu' calls.

. . . . . . . . . . . . . . . . . . .

# CHAPTER FIVE

# FINDING FOOD

**COMMON BEE-EATER**
*(Merops apiaster)*

NIGHTJARS WHEEL AND TWIST *in the air, using their enormous bills like butterfly nets to catch swarms of mosquitos or even giant moths; small flocks of emus optimistically follow clouds in the hope of finding fruit, insects or other food wherever it has rained; and strange secretary birds nervously kill tasty snakes by stamping on them. There are very few plants or small animals in the world that are beyond the reach of one bird or another.*

*Such variety in their diet requires a wide range of different feeding techniques. Birds have no hands, so they must catch and hold food with their bills alone. Parrots, birds of prey, owls and some other species are able to use their feet as well, but even they have bills appropriate to their food. Owls have short, hooked bills for tearing up their prey, oystercatchers have bills for smashing through mussels and cockle shells, while skimmers have extended lower mandibles that they use to scoop up fish from just below the water's surface.*

**PIED FLYCATCHER**
*(Ficedula hypoleuca)*

*A unique example is the now-extinct huia from New Zealand. A large, crow-sized bird, it was predominantly black except for a bright-orange 'wattle' on either side of its face. Male and female huias were once thought to be separate species because their bills were so different. The male's was short and starling-like for breaking up rotten bark in search of insects, while the female's was long and curved for picking up any insects hiding in crevices that the male could not reach. Sadly, this extraordinary bird became extinct at the beginning of this century.*

However, a well-designed bill is not enough. Birds also require suitable forms of behaviour to find, catch and then eat their food.

A peregrine falcon can spot a pigeon at a distance of several miles. When it dives on to it from a great height, the unsuspecting bird is knocked to the ground with the force of the impact. Owls have a similar but rather more subtle approach; their feathers have fringed edges to muffle the sound of their wingbeats as they swoop on to small animals in the darkness.

Digesting the food can be a problem, because birds do not have teeth. Some have evolved serrations on the sides of their bills which are very similar. Mergansers use these for catching and holding on to slippery fish. But even the best bills cannot chew.

Many birds break up their food with the help of a gizzard. This is a special muscular portion of the stomach which grinds the food into a pulp. Birds which eat comparatively soft food, such as fish, meat or insects, can manage with strong digestive juices. But seed-eaters and other birds relying on food that is more difficult to break down need to swallow pieces of grit to help their gizzards with the digestion. Willow ptarmigans have long claws specially designed to scratch through the winter snow and reach the grit underneath.

Any completely indigestible parts, such as shell fragments, fur, bones or beetles' wings, are coughed up in the form of tightly packed pellets.

Many birds also have a sac-like enlargement of the gullet, called the crop, which is used somewhat like a shopping basket. Some species use it to carry food to their nestlings but, more importantly, it enables many birds to gorge themselves very quickly before hiding away in a safe place to digest their food in peace.

**GREY HERON**
*(Ardea cinerea)*

**GENTOO PENGUIN**
*(Pygoscelis papua)*

**LITTLE WATTLEBIRD**
*(Anthochaera chrysoptera)*

ABOVE: **S**ome plants in Australia intentionally produce only a few flowers at a time to force the birds that feed on their nectar to be nomadic. This ensures adequate cross-fertilization, since the birds get covered in pollen while feeding and have to move from plant to plant. One of these nectar-eating birds is the little wattlebird, a kind of honeyeater found in a variety of woodland and scrubland habitats in southern Australia and Tasmania. Like other members of the family, it eats insects as well as nectar, and these provide important nutrients that are unobtainable from nectar alone. Wattlebirds are named for the fleshy pieces of skin that hang from the sides of their bills, although in the little wattlebird these are minute and almost invisible.

. . . . . . . . . . . . . . . . . . . . .

**GILA WOODPECKER**
*(Melanerpes uropygialis)*

RIGHT: **G**ila woodpeckers are conspicuous birds in the scrub desert and cactus country of the south-western United States and Mexico. With the help of their strong claws, short legs and stiff tails, they clamber all over giant cacti in search of insects. They even bore their nesting cavities in the cacti and, when abandoned, these are often used by other birds. Sparrow-sized elf owls *(Micrathene whitneyi)* are frequent occupants: they use the holes for both nesting and roosting. Sometimes an owl and a woodpecker may share the same cavity. The owl sleeps in the hole by day, moving out for its nightly hunting expedition when the woodpecker comes home to roost at dusk. Only the male gila woodpecker has the red cap that is clearly visible in this picture.

. . . . . . . . . . . . . . . . . . . . .

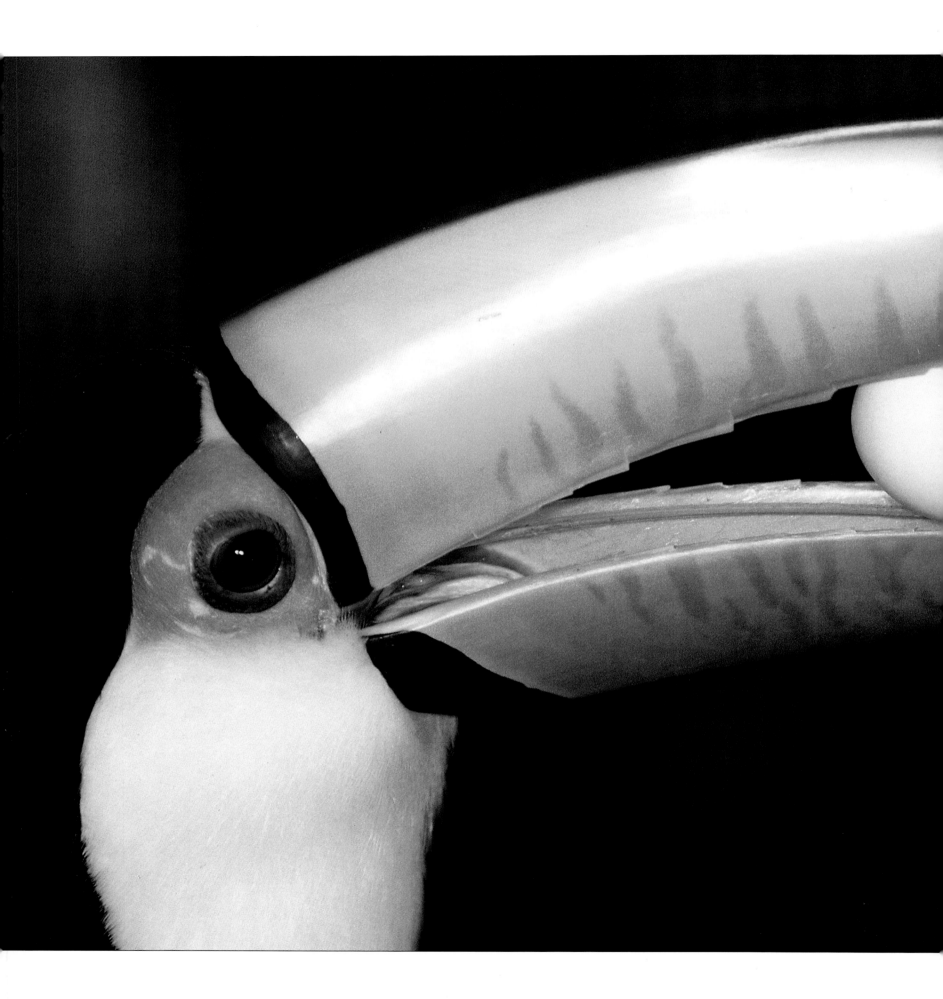

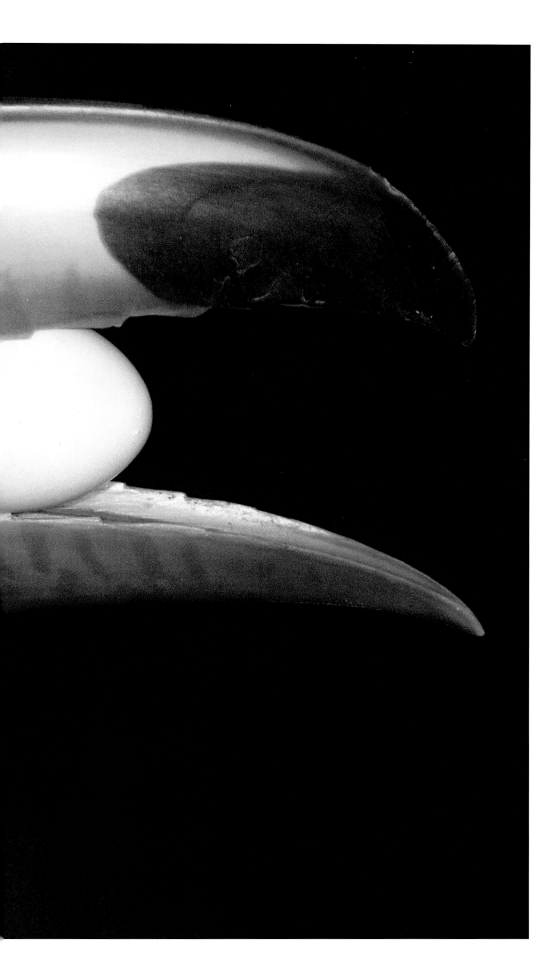

### EGYPTIAN VULTURE
### *(Neophron percnopterus)*

ABOVE: **E**gyptian vultures are last in the vulturine pecking order
around a carcass and usually end up with just the scraps.
However, they consume a variety of other food to supplement
their diets – including birds' eggs. The eggs of pelicans and
flamingos are broken by being hurled against rocks, while ostrich
eggs are cracked open by having large stones dropped on to
them. Found on the open plains of southern Europe, Africa, the
Middle East and parts of Asia, Egyptian vultures are more
attractive than most members of the family because they have
feathers on their heads and necks, only their faces being bare.

. . . . . . . . . . . . . . . . . . . .

### TOCO TOUCAN
### *(Ramphastos toco)*

LEFT: **T**he toco toucan is the largest member of the toucan
family, with an enormous beak some 8 in (20 cm) long. Despite
its size, the beak is surprisingly light, and it seems to have a
number of different uses. It is long enough to enable the bird to
pluck distant fruit that would otherwise be out of reach; it is
sometimes used to intimidate potential predators; and it may also
be important in courtship. Toco toucans live in the rain forests of
eastern South America. They are bold and mischievous birds
that often enter houses to steal food or to torment pet cats and
dogs. They have a varied diet, which includes fruits, eggs,
nestlings, lizards and insects. The bird in this picture
has stolen a pigeon's egg.

. . . . . . . . . . . . . . . . . . . .

### RESPLENDENT QUETZAL
*(Pharomachrus mocino)*

ABOVE AND LEFT: The quetzal is such an extraordinary bird that its very existence was doubted for many years. A spectacular emerald and crimson colour, it has beautiful tail feathers, up to 24 in (61 cm) in length, which are shed and re-grown after each breeding season. Its favourite food is laurel fruit, which is what the bird in the main picture is about to swallow whole; it will regurgitate the large stone later. The quetzal also eats a variety of other fruits and berries, lizards, small frogs, insects and snails. It inhabits the mountain jungles of Central America.

. . . . . . . . . . . . . . . . . . . .

### RAINBOW LORIKEET
*(Trichoglossus haematodus)*

RIGHT: Rainbow lorikeets are noisy birds that continually screech and chatter as they clamber among the foliage in search of food. Their varied diet includes seeds and insect larvae, and their predilection for ripening soft fruit makes them unpopular visitors to orchards. But the birds eat mainly pollen and nectar, which they mop up with the help of brush-like tips on their long tongues. Rainbow lorikeets are also called blue mountain parrots, or blueys, and they inhabit wooded areas of South-east Asia and Australia. In suburban areas they become quite tame and can be hand-fed with nectar and other titbits.

. . . . . . . . . . . . . . . . . . . .

### BALD EAGLE
*(Haliaeetus leucocephalus)*

ABOVE: **T**he North American bald eagle is well known as the
national emblem of the United States of America. Despite its
fame, it has declined alarmingly in recent years due to
pressure from hunting, habitat disturbance and chemical
pesticides. Named after its striking white head and neck, it is an
impressive bird, with a wingspan of more than 8 ft (2.5 m). Bald
eagles live along remote coasts, or near rivers and lakes in
wilderness areas. They feed mainly on dead and dying fish, often
wading into cold, salmon-spawning rivers to catch the tired
animals in the shallows. They also catch live fish by swooping
low over the water and snatching them up with their huge talons.
Being opportunists, they take a variety of other prey and, as
shown in this picture, will even feed on carrion.

. . . . . . . . . . . . . . . . . . . .

### WHITE-BELLIED SEA EAGLE
*(Haliaeetus leucogaster)*

RIGHT: **W**hite-bellied sea eagles glide low over the water, then
drop on to their prey feet-first, usually with such force that their
talons kill the fish instantly. During the dry season, when water
levels are low, they find fishing particularly easy. The immature
bird in this picture has just caught a fish and is flying to a safe
perch to eat its meal. White-bellied sea eagles are common birds
in many parts of Australia and Asia, in a range stretching from
India to the Solomon Islands. Despite their spectacular, 6.5 ft
(2 m) wingspans, they are relatively small for eagles. They live
along coasts, including some built-up areas such as Sydney
Harbour, as well as inland on large rivers, swamps, lakes and
reservoirs.

. . . . . . . . . . . . . . . . . . . .

## HOUSE SPARROW
### (Passer domesticus)

RIGHT: **T**hese birds are seldom far from human habitation and appear to prefer built-up areas to the countryside. They have followed people virtually all over the world, even travelling with them on trains, ships and ferries. They are inventive opportunists, although they have an inbuilt mistrust of people that prevents them from taking irresponsible risks. House sparrows will eat almost anything, but seem to prefer seeds, insects and bread. The bird in this picture is a rather drab female; the more striking male has a grey crown and smart black bib.

. . . . . . . . . . . . . . . . . . . .

## SONG THRUSH
### (Turdus philomelos)

TOP OPPOSITE: **A** song thrush's ability to crack open a snail's shell is almost legendary. Using a stone as an anvil, it hammers the snail until the shell breaks and it can get at the juicy meal inside. Favoured stones, often known as 'workshops', are littered with discarded shells and are a familiar sight in woods, parks and gardens throughout many parts of the world. Depending on the time of year, song thrushes will also eat earthworms, insects, berries and fruit. They prefer to feed on the ground and, even when frequenting a bird table, will normally hunt around its base rather than on the table itself. Song thrushes are found in Europe, North Africa and parts of Asia, and have been introduced into Australia and New Zealand.

. . . . . . . . . . . . . . . . . . . .

### ROBIN
#### (Erithacus rubecula)

ABOVE RIGHT: **R**obins are shy, skulking woodland birds in many parts of their range in Europe, North Africa and Asia. However, they do become very tame in some areas and have a habit of boldly picking up earthworms, spiders and insects around a gardener's feet as he turns over the soil. They cannot resist mealworms and will often risk feeding from people's hands in order to get them. In the winter, they look much larger than at other times of the year because they fluff out their feathers to keep warm.

. . . . . . . . . . . . . . . . . . . .

### BLACKBIRD
#### (Turdus merula)

BOTTOM RIGHT: **B**lackbirds are particularly fond of berries and will often gorge themselves in suitable bushes; the bird in this picture is feeding on hawthorn. More commonly, however, a blackbird will feed on the ground. It moves about in short, hopping runs, then pauses for a moment and turns its head to one side as if listening for something. In fact, it is looking for the tell-tale movements of a worm or insect. Blackbirds are common in Europe, North Africa and parts of Asia, and have been introduced into Australia and New Zealand.

. . . . . . . . . . . . . . . . . . . .

### COMMON BUZZARD
*(Buteo buteo)*

ABOVE: **B**uzzards are very adaptable birds
that are able to adjust their hunting methods
to suit the kind of prey available. They prefer
open country with scattered trees, and will
perch on a suitable vantage point for hours
looking for small, ground-dwelling mammals.
They are able to soar and hover, and can
tackle anything up to the size of a rabbit.
Voles and other small creatures are swallowed
whole, but larger prey is torn to pieces with
their strong, hooked beaks. Sometimes they
wait on roadside telegraph poles for road
casualties, or walk about on the ground
looking for earthworms and beetles. Known in
Africa as steppe buzzards, common buzzards
are also found in many parts of Europe
and Asia.

. . . . . . . . . . . . . . . . . . . .

### RED-SHOULDERED HAWK
*(Buteo lineatus)*

RIGHT: **T**he red-shouldered hawk is a noisy
and conspicuous bird around its nesting area
in the spring. For the rest of the year it tends
to remain fairly well hidden. The bird rarely
hunts on the wing, preferring to search for its
prey from a low tree perch in a wooded river
valley or similar area with trees and water. It
lives in parts of North America and Mexico,
and takes a wide variety of prey. Snakes are a
particular favourite, especially in the
summer, but it will also take rodents, frogs,
small birds and large insects.

. . . . . . . . . . . . . . . . . . . .

### AFRICAN GREY PARROT
*(Psittacus erithacus)*

LEFT: **P**arrots are either left-footed or right-footed. They use their feet like hands, to grasp food and to hold it steady for eating. Climbing from branch to branch in the treetops, African grey parrots search for seeds, nuts, berries and fruit, a particular favourite being the fruit of the oil palm. They live in the rain forests of West, Central and East Africa, and are probably the best mimics of all parrots which, unfortunately, has made them popular cage-birds. Recent experiments have demonstrated that they do not always learn words 'parrot-fashion' – without understanding their meaning – but may be capable of using them for actual communication.

. . . . . . . . . . . . . . . . . . .

### VERREAUX'S EAGLE OWL
*(Bubo lacteus)*

ABOVE: **T**he Verreaux's eagle owl hunts almost exclusively at night. It has excellent hearing and exceptionally keen eyesight, with a light-gathering power many times that of our own. Its wing feathers have softened edges, which means that its flight is virtually noiseless, and it is a large and powerful bird. Able to pinpoint its prey accurately, and to glide silently down from its perch, it catches animals as large as vervet monkeys with relative ease. This owl has a particular penchant for hedgehogs, but will take almost anything, from roosting birds and flying insects to frogs and fruit bats. The bird is well distributed in the woodlands and savannas of Africa, especially where there are rivers. Also known as the milky eagle owl, or giant eagle owl, it measures up to 2 ft (65 cm) in length.

. . . . . . . . . . . . . . . . . . .

**COSTA'S HUMMINGBIRD**
*(Calypte costae)* ABOVE
**RUFOUS HUMMINGBIRD**
*(Selasphorus rufus)* BELOW
**BROAD-BILLED HUMMINGBIRD**
*(Cynanthus latirostris)* RIGHT

**A** hummingbird's wings beat up and down as many as 80 times
every second. They move so swiftly that they are visible only as
a blur, making the strange humming sound that gives the bird its
name. Hovering motionless in mid-air with immaculate
precision, a hummingbird can hold its position in front of a
flower while it drinks the nectar inside. The longest bill of all
belongs to the swordbill hummingbird *(Ensifera ensifera)*: 4 in
(10.5 cm) in length, it is designed to reach into the bottom of a
particularly deep species of passion flower. Hummingbirds have
extendable, tube-like tongues, which are used like straws to
suck up nectar. While they are feeding, their faces and bills
become dusted with pollen and, as they move from flower to
flower, they help to cross-pollinate the plants. The birds use up
a great deal of energy in flight, so they need tremendous amounts
of food. Most eat and drink over half their body-weights every
day, often supplementing their nectar diet with small insects.
There are 315 species altogether, and the majority are beautifully
coloured in irridescent greens, blues, purples, reds and yellows.
They live mainly in Central and South America, although a
number also occur in North America.

. . . . . . . . . . . . . . . . . . . .

### BLACK GUILLEMOT
#### *(Cepphus grylle)*

ABOVE: **B**lack guillemots and other members of the auk family
are the northern equivalents of the penguins. However, the two
groups are not closely related and their resemblance is the result
of adaptation to similar conditions. The most obvious difference
between the two groups is that auks can fly and penguins cannot.

Also known as tysties or sea pigeons, black guillemots feed
mainly near the sea bottom, preferring shallow water to depths of
about 130 ft (40 m). Like penguins, they 'fly' underwater in
pursuit of their prey, which consists of fish, crustaceans,
molluscs and marine worms. The bird in this picture is in its
striking summer plumage; in winter, much of the black fades to
grey and white.

. . . . . . . . . . . . . . . . . . . .

### JACKASS PENGUIN
#### *(Spheniscus demersus)*

LEFT: **E**very morning, jackass penguins leave their island-based
roosts or breeding colonies to spend all day fishing in the wild,
tempestuous seas off the southern tip of Africa. Supreme
swimmers and divers, they forage in small groups in the
comparatively shallow waters over the continental shelf. When
pursuing squid and fast-moving fish such as pilchards and
anchovies, their dives frequently last for two minutes, and they
can stay underwater for as long as five minutes. Ninety per cent
of the total world population of jackass penguins has been lost
since the beginning of this century, bringing the total down from
millions to around 150,000. Guano collection and egg collecting
for food continued on a massive scale until the 1960s. In recent
years, major oil spills and the development of highly efficient sea
fisheries have added to the pressures.

. . . . . . . . . . . . . . . . . . . .

### WHITE STORK
### *(Ciconia ciconia)*

LEFT: **W**hite storks are popular birds that are welcomed in towns and villages all over Europe, where they breed on chimney stacks and rooftops. People often erect cartwheels and other platforms to help the birds find suitable bases for their enormous nests. The storks pay their rent by eating rodents and by scavenging, although they also feed on frogs, fish, insects and earthworms. On their African wintering grounds, they are affectionately known as 'grasshopper birds' because they have a habit of following locust swarms and gorging themselves on the plentiful insects. Hunting in Africa, pesticide poisoning and changing agricultural practices have all led to a decline in white stork populations in recent years.

. . . . . . . . . . . . . . . . . . .

### AMERICAN AVOCET
### *(Recurvirostra americana)*

RIGHT: **A**vocets are among the few birds that have upcurved bills. These are long and slender, and are swept from side to side in search of crustaceans, insect larvae, tadpoles, small fish and other aquatic animals. In deeper water, the birds will swim rather than wade, up-ending to find their food. American avocets live around shallow ponds, marshes, lake shores and coastal flats in North and Central America. The bird in this picture is in breeding plumage; towards the end of the summer, it will lose the rusty colouring as its head and neck turn pale grey.

. . . . . . . . . . . . . . . . . . .

### BLACK-HEADED HERON
*(Ardea melanocephala)*

ABOVE: **A**lthough it is a wading bird, the black-headed heron generally prefers to hunt rodents, insects and small birds on pasture land and in other dry areas. But it takes a wide variety of prey, including frogs, crabs and fish, and so frequents marshes and coastal waters as well. The bird in this picture is wandering slowly through the grass, but black-headed herons often hunt by standing motionless and looking for tell-tale movements. They are common residents in Africa south of the Sahara.

. . . . . . . . . . . . . . . . . . . .

### GREAT BLUE HERON
*(Ardea herodias)*

LEFT: **T**he great blue heron is the New World equivalent of the grey heron. It is found around the lakes, ponds, rivers and marshes of North and Central America and northern South America. As it stands motionless in the water, or walks slowly through the shallows, it is ready to strike at a fish with lightning speed. It also eats frogs and will take a variety of other prey, from snakes and lizards to insects and turtle hatchlings.

. . . . . . . . . . . . . . . . . . . .

### LAVA HERON
*(Butorides sundevalli)*

RIGHT: **T**he lava heron is endemic to the Galapagos Islands. Although it is thought by many experts to be a distinct species, others consider it to be just a variety of the more widespread striated heron *(Butorides striatus)*. It is a familiar sight along the shorelines of all the islands in the group, as it hunts for small crabs and lizards among the rocks, and for fish in the tidal creeks. It also perches among the roots of mangrove swamps, and dives into the water to catch small fry; it will even pick flies off dead animals. The bird stretching its head and neck forward in this photograph is probably taking aim at a fish.

. . . . . . . . . . . . . . . . . . . .

### GREEN HERON
*(Butorides virescens)*

BELOW: **T**he green heron looks more blue than green from a distance, although its back is a light greyish-green. It lives in tropical and sub-tropical North, Central and South America, preferring wetland habitats with thick bushes or trees nearby. It hunts by crouching motionless for long periods before catching its prey with a rapid jab.

. . . . . . . . . . . . . . . . . . . .

**BROWN PELICAN**
*(Pelecanus occidentalis)*

The brown pelican is the smallest of the world's pelicans and
rather different from other members of the group. A marine
species found in many parts of North and South America, it feeds
exclusively by diving for fish (all other pelicans feed from the
water's surface). When diving, it folds its wings to increase the
falling speed and hurtles down into the sea, sometimes from a
height of 50 ft (15 m) or more. Contrary to popular opinion, its
pouch is not used to store fish but is designed as a net to catch
them. Excess water is strained off and the fish are swallowed
soon after being caught. Since the patch of skin underneath the
bill is naked, it may also help to keep the bird cool.

. . . . . . . . . . . . . . . . . . .

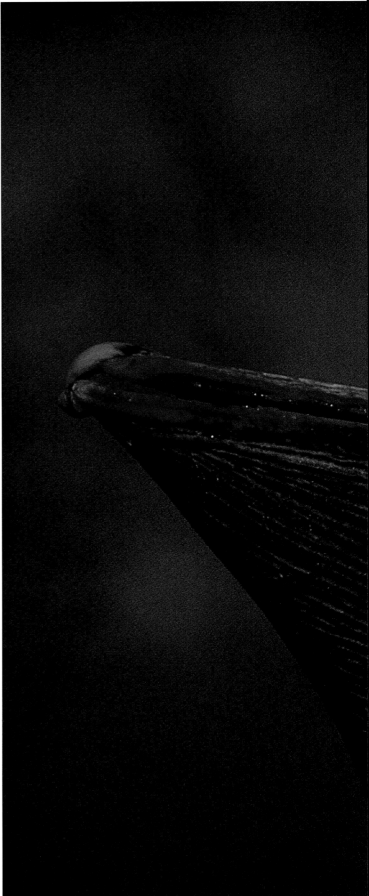

### ROSEATE SPOONBILL
### (Platalea ajaja)

LEFT: The roseate spoonbill feeds by touch rather than by sight. It wades in shallow water, swinging its open bill from side to side, ready to snap it shut as soon as it encounters something in the mud. Its bill is distinctive – and looks rather ridiculous – with a broad, flattened, spoon-shaped tip. In fact, it is a highly efficient feeding instrument designed to catch slow-moving or bottom-dwelling shrimps and fish. The bill is sensitive to the slightest vibration, and enables the bird to feed in muddy water where it would be impossible for it to hunt by sight. Roseate spoonbills live in parts of North, Central and South America.

. . . . . . . . . . . . . . . . . . . .

### PAINTED STORK
### (Ibis leucocephalus)

ABOVE: The painted stork is viewed with as much affection in its native south and South-east Asia as the white stork is in Europe. It is a familiar sight hunting for fish on marshes, lakes and paddyfields. Wading in the shallows, with its half-opened bill ploughing through the water, it can hunt by sight but, like the roseate spoonbill, normally uses touch. Its long, tapering, decurved bill snaps shut within a fraction of a second of sensing a fish. Painted storks often travel considerable distances to reach suitable feeding sites, flying up to high altitudes before gliding away.

. . . . . . . . . . . . . . . . . . . .

### COMMON TERN
### (Sterna hirundo)

LEFT: **W**hen hunting, common terns fly in small flocks a few feet above the water. They hover briefly over fish clearly visible near the surface before plunging in with a splash and seizing them in their bills. Their favourite food is whitebait, but they eat a variety of other small fish and even insects, which are caught both over water and on land. Common terns breed across a wide band in the northern hemisphere; many individuals migrate to the southern hemisphere for the winter. Their range overlaps with that of the Arctic tern, which looks very similar. In a mixed flock seen at a distance the two species can be virtually indistinguishable, so frustrated ornithologists sometimes dub them 'comic' terns.

. . . . . . . . . . . . . . . . . . . .

### GREAT BLACK-BACKED GULL
### (Larus marinus)

RIGHT: **T**he great black-backed gull is a huge, powerful and formidable bird, weighing up to 4.4 lb (2 kg) and with a wingspan of more than 5 ft (1.5 m). It will eat almost anything: offal discarded by fishing boats, eggs, fish, carrion and rodents. It also kills and eats animals as large as puffins and rabbits, scavenges on inland refuse tips, swallows nestlings (even those of its own species) in one gulp, and chases other seabirds, forcing them to disgorge their food. Found along the coasts of the North Atlantic and Arctic, this menacing bird is the largest of all the gulls.

. . . . . . . . . . . . . . . . . . . .

## KINGFISHER
### (Alcedo atthis)

ABOVE AND OPPOSITE: **A** flash of brilliant electric blue is usually all you see of a kingfisher as it dashes past. Flying like an arrow, low over the water, it is probably heading for its next perch along the riverbank. If the bird spots a fish on the way, it can brake in mid-air and hover overhead. However, it prefers to hunt while sitting motionless on a branch that overhangs the water. Once it has located a small fish near the surface, the kingfisher tenses for a moment before diving. It actually flies downwards, rather than drops, and by the time it plunges head-first into the water, it is moving at a considerable speed. It makes a few last-second adjustments to its aim underwater, and then seizes the fish in its dagger-like bill. With strong wingbeats, and clenching its prey firmly in its beak, the kingfisher struggles free of the water. If it has chicks to feed, a successful hunter may fly straight to the nesting burrow, which will be situated in a nearby riverbank. Otherwise it will return to its fishing perch to beat the fish before swallowing it head-first. In recent years, kingfishers have disappeared from many parts of their former range in Europe, North Africa and Asia. They are particularly susceptible to hard winters, but also suffer from human disturbance and pollution.

. . . . . . . . . . . . . . . . . . . .

CLOCKWISE FROM TOP LEFT:
**PIED KINGFISHER**
*(Ceryle rudis)*
**GIANT KINGFISHER**
*(Ceryle maxima)*
**AZURE KINGFISHER**
*(Ceyx azureus)*
**MALACHITE
KINGFISHER**
*(Alcedo cristata)*
**STRIPED KINGFISHER**
*(Halcyon chelicuti)*

# CHAPTER SIX

# OUT TO IMPRESS

. . . . . . . . . . . . . . . . . .

**SHARP-TAILED GROUSE**
*(Tympanuchus
phasianellus)*

**PEACOCK**
*(Pavo cristatus)* RIGHT

WRENS MOBBING A TAWNY OWL *at its roost, great tits spreading their wings and tail feathers in a dispute over food and a ringed plover feigning injury to lead a predator away from its nest: all of these are examples of the many rites and rituals that birds use for communication. However, it is the need to find a partner and reproduce that has re-sulted in the most impressive displays of all.*

*Typically, the male is the more active partner during court-ship, but almost every conceivable matrimonial agreement exists somewhere in the bird world. Some males are faithful to their partners for life, others are terribly promiscuous and mate with as many females as they can, abandoning them in succession. The phalaropes even reverse the usual roles of the sexes: the females court the males and leave them to care for their young.*

*In the breeding season, male birds which are normally shy and retiring begin to strive for attention. With their loud voices, bright colours and eye-catching displays, they establish and defend territories, challenge their rivals and go out of their way to attract females. They often become so obsessed with showing off to their contemporaries that they do little else.*

*Some of the most impressive displays are given by birds of paradise. Many brightly plumaged males of the 40 known species inhabiting the rain forests of New Guinea, the Moluccan Islands and northern Australia have long tail and head feathers and irridescent colours that stand out sharply against the dark forest background. They hang upside-down, vibrate their wings, spread their feathers out in graceful curves, bow, dance and shriek to attract their mates.*

**EASTERN MEADOWLARK**
*(Sturnella magna)* LEFT

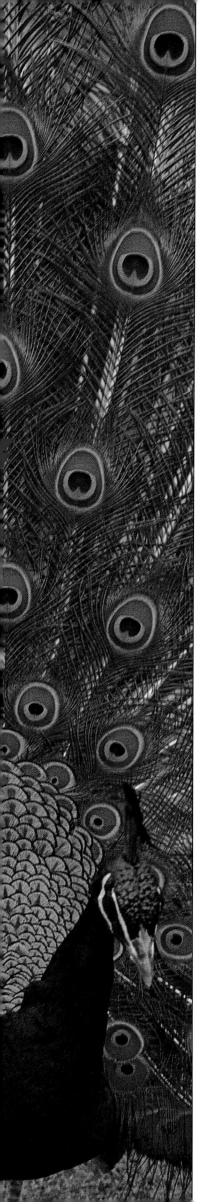

Many other brightly coloured and bold birds use a similar combination of visual signals and ritual behaviour in their courtship displays. Bald eagles and other birds of prey use their considerable flying skills for displays in which they lock talons in mid-air and somersault through the skies together. Peacocks raise their enormous tails and prance and strut in front of the females, while male ruffs develop large ear-tufts and frills of feathers around their necks to impress their potential mates and to intimidate one another.

Ruffs are among many birds which prefer to remain inconspicuous for most of the year. They put on a bright plumage specially for the breeding season and change to a duller one for the winter.

Some species dare not show themselves even during courtship. They do not have colourful adornments and eye-catching displays, and are rather drab and well-camouflaged birds that prefer to remain hidden in the trees and bushes. But there may be so many drab birds in an area that the females sometimes have trouble in recognising their own species. The males therefore have distinctive voices. Unlike their florid cousins, who generally have short and unattractive calls, they use long, elaborate songs to pronounce their intentions. The females can distinguish sounds much closer in time than we can – a single note to us may be several separate notes to them – and therefore have no trouble in identifying and locating suitable mates.

**SEVEN-COLOURED TANAGER**
*(Tangara fastuosa)*

**DIPPER**
*(Cinclus cinclus)*

### COMMON GANNET
*(Sula bassana)*

ABOVE: There may be as many as 25,000 pairs in a single gannet
colony on a rock or island in the North Atlantic. The birds are so
densely packed that life in the colony is very competitive. The
two limiting factors are food and space: 50,000 adults and their
chicks require nearly 50 tons of fish every day and each pair
continually has to defend a small territory around its nest. The
birds become so aggressive that they need to make special
displays to ensure that the aggression which they show towards
their neighbours is not unleashed on their partners. The pair of
birds in this picture is engaged in a form of activity known as
'mutual fencing', which is a type of greeting designed specifically
to reduce aggression and fear.

. . . . . . . . . . . . . . . . . . . .

### ANDEAN FLAMINGO
*(Phoenicoparrus andinus)*

RIGHT: Glorious pink feathers are important to the breeding
success of flamingos. The colour is not natural and fades
gradually in the sunlight until the feathers are almost white. In
the wild the pigment comes from the little crustaceans that the
flamingos eat, but zoos have to provide it artificially by adding
carotene to the flamingos' food. Andean flamingos have a
courtship display that appears to consist of everyday preening
and stretching movements. However, these movements are in
predictable sequences and tend to be a little stiffer than normal,
with a few ballet-like steps added for good measure. The display
is very infectious and, as shown in this picture, when one
member of a group starts, the others cannot resist joining in.

. . . . . . . . . . . . . . . . . . .

### BLACK-NECKED RED COTINGA
#### (Phoenicircus nigricollis)

RIGHT: The cotingas are a very diverse group of birds that are closely related to the manakins and to the huge American family of tyrant flycatchers. There are nearly 70 different species, all of which live in tropical Mexico and Central and South America. The males of many cotingas are brilliantly coloured and they have very elaborate courtship displays. The short-winged, heavily built bird in this picture is a male, photographed on his display perch in the Amazon rain forest of Peru.

. . . . . . . . . . . . . . . . . . .

### WIRE-TAILED MANAKIN
#### (Pipra filicauda)

ABOVE: Male wire-tailed manakins put on a sensational show for their females in the thick, lowland rain forests of northern South America. Each bird begins by selecting a branch on which to display, and then removes all the leaves that might interfere with his performance. The show opens with a conspicuous and dramatic landing on the chosen perch, and continues with a variety of spectacular slides, twists and pirouettes. As a grand finale, the performer turns around and tickles the female under her chin with his long, wire-like tail feathers. She succumbs and goes away to lay her eggs and raise their young alone, while the male enacts a repeat performance for his next female visitor.

. . . . . . . . . . . . . . . . . . .

### GREATER FRIGATEBIRD
#### (Fregata minor)

RIGHT: Courting greater frigatebirds must rank among the most extraordinary sights on remote tropical islands in the South Atlantic, Pacific and Indian Oceans. The adult males sit in noisy gatherings on the trees or shrubs in which they plan to nest. They have incredible scarlet throat patches which they keep inflated like balloons for many hours. As soon as a female flies into view all the males start showing off in the hope of winning her favours. Vibrating their open wings, they throw back and vigorously shake their heads to draw attention to the throat patches, and call or clack their bills. It is a spectacular performance that the female cannot resist. She hovers overhead before making her choice and finally drops down beside her new mate.

. . . . . . . . . . . . . . . . . . .

### ARCTIC SKUA
#### *(Stercorarius parasiticus)*

ABOVE: **A**rctic skuas, or parasitic jaegers as they are known in North America, are the pirates of the Arctic tundra. They chase and torment other seabirds to rob them of their food, and plunder their nests to eat the eggs and young. However, they take great exception to intruders around their own nest-sites and ferociously attack humans with fast, swooping dives aimed at the head. Although contact is rarely made, this can be an unnerving experience. The birds in the picture are feigning injury – their behaviour is known as the 'broken wing distraction display' – to draw the photographer away from their eggs, which are located in a scrape in the ground.

.....................

### PUFFIN
#### *(Fratercula arctica)*

LEFT: **P**uffins are sociable birds and spend hours loafing around together outside their home-made nesting burrows on the grassy slopes of offshore islands. The burrows are lined with feathers and bits of grass, which the puffins collect throughout the summer – but the birds are so full of energy that they sometimes make these collections purely for fun. The bird in this picture, which was photographed in the Faroe Islands, waddled over with a beak-full of grass and placed it carefully on the ground just in front of the photographer. Puffins are comical and naturally inquisitive birds that show little fear of people at their breeding colonies in the North Atlantic and Arctic Oceans. Their brightly coloured, parrot-like bills, which are brightest during the breeding season in early summer, play an important role in pair-formation and courtship as well as in catching fish.

.....................

### JAPANESE CRANE
*(Grus japonensis)*

**J**apanese cranes are enthusiastic dancers. They leap into the air, flap their wings, throw their heads back and bob them up and down, bow deeply, run around and even do a bit of flying. Also known as Manchurian or red-crowned cranes, they actually seem to dance for pleasure, and when one member of the flock decides to take to the floor the others cannot resist joining in. However, dancing also plays an important role in the birds' lives. Young cranes dance together as a way of getting to know each other and, if an established pair is going through a bad patch, dancing helps to strengthen their bond. Japanese cranes have never been particularly numerous and have come under increasing pressure from the destruction of their wetland habitats as well as, in recent years, from collisions with overhead electric power cables. As a consequence, their population has plummeted to a dangerously low level, with fewer than 1,000 survivors living in China, Japan, North and South Korea and the USSR.

. . . . . . . . . . . . . . . . . . . .

### GREAT BOWERBIRD
*(Chlamydera nuchalis)* ABOVE
### SATIN BOWERBIRD
*(Ptilonorhynchus violaceus)* RIGHT

**M**ale bowerbirds go to great lengths to impress the females. In their forest homes in Australia and New Guinea, they spend many months building and maintaining ornate 'bowers' on the ground. These vary in design, depending on the species, from simple clearings and avenues of grass to substantial roofed huts. Over the years, the birds gain experience and are able to perfect their building techniques. Sometimes the bowers are painted with berry juice and makeshift paintbrushes. They are all liberally decorated with bright objects such as berries, flowers, mushrooms, stones, tin foil or glass. There is great rivalry between the males and they often steal sought-after objects from each other's collections. Satin bowerbirds are particularly fond of anything blue and the male in the picture on the right has selected a blue plastic lid. The great bowerbird prefers rounded objects such as shells, bones and even kangaroo droppings. Generally speaking, the duller the male is, the more elaborate is his bower – apparently to make up for his own shortcomings – and there appears to be a correlation between the colour of his plumage and that of the treasures he collects. When a female begins to show interest, the male cackles and dances around, carefully displaying his decorations as if showing her valuable jewels. If all goes well, they mate inside or near the bower, and the female then goes away to build a nest, incubate her eggs and raise the young on her own. Meanwhile, the male is trying to attract more females into his parlour.

. . . . . . . . . . . . . . . . . . .

### SKYLARK
#### *(Alauda arvensis)*

RIGHT: **S**kylarks do not like trees. They prefer open country, and sing their loud, warbling songs from fenceposts, from the ground or, more commonly, from the air. They hang in the sky for up to five minutes at a time, so high that they are virtually out of sight, and their singing can be heard for miles around. When advertising for a mate, or warning other skylarks to stay away from their territories, two rivals will sometimes sing against one another in adjacent fields. Their flight over, they drop slowly towards the ground, singing as they go, until their final, silent, descent. Skylarks are widely distributed in Europe, Asia and North Africa, and have been introduced into Australasia and Canada.

. . . . . . . . . . . . . . . . . . . .

### CROWNED PLOVER
#### (Vanellus coronatus)

LEFT: **T**he noisy cries of the crowned plover can be heard across the short, grassy plains and open bush country of many parts of southern and East Africa. It repeats its scolding 'yik-yik' or chattering 'tri-tri-tri' calls all day long and often throughout the night as well. Crowned plovers are not strongly territorial and often nest in loose colonies, but they are particularly noisy during the breeding season. They have highly vocal courtship displays and protect their chicks by dive-bombing intruders and screaming loudly.

. . . . . . . . . . . . . . . . . . .

### YELLOWHAMMER
#### (Emberiza citrinella)

ABOVE: **W**hen defending his territory against rival birds, the male yellowhammer throws back his head, opens his bill wide and utters a song which sounds as if he is saying 'little-piece-of-bread-and-no-----cheese'. A familiar sound in many parts of Europe and Asia, it is evocative but, at the same time, rather monotonous – simply the rapid repetition of the same note, with a slight variation at the end. In some parts of the yellowhammer's range, including New Zealand, where the species has been introduced with some success, it tends to omit the 'cheese' at the beginning and end of the singing season. The song is usually uttered from an exposed perch on farmland or from the top of a hedge.

. . . . . . . . . . . . . . . . . . .

## SAGE GROUSE
### *(Centrocercus urophasianus)*

TOP, FAR LEFT: **S**trange sounds can sometimes be heard in the sagebrush regions of western North America. These are made by male sage grouse gathering in their hundreds at traditional courting grounds calls 'leks'. Each bird defends a small plot from which he displays to visiting females. He raises and fans his tail, rapidly inflates and deflates the huge air sacs that hang down his chest and, at the same time, emits a loud, deep, bubbling call. Visiting females are usually so impressed with the display that they head straight for the centre of the lek and mate with the most dominant males.

. . . . . . . . . . . . . . . . . . .

## BLACK-BELLIED BUSTARD
### *(Eupodotis melanogaster)*

LEFT: **D**uring the breeding season, the male black-bellied bustard makes impressive display flights, using slow, exaggerated wingbeats, and then gliding to the ground with his chest puffed out. Known in Africa as the black-bellied korhaan, this bird also has a very strange song. It begins with a hoarse call and ends with a sound like a cork popping from its bottle, and is repeated several times a minute. The bird in this picture is a male; the female lacks the black belly which gives the species its name.

. . . . . . . . . . . . . . . . . . .

## KORI BUSTARD
### *(Ardeotis kori)*

RIGHT: **T**he heaviest flying birds in the world are the great bustard and the kori bustard. Kori bustards stand up to 5 ft (1.5 m) tall and weigh from 30 lb (13.5 kg) to an astonishing 42 lb (19 kg). Some individuals are so heavy that they are barely able to get off the ground. They are common birds in Africa, and can be seen strolling sedately around the grasslands and savannas, looking rather snooty with their bills pointing slightly skyward. The male of the species has a spectacular courtship display. Standing upright, he folds his tail up and over his back and inflates his neck like a balloon. The feathers on his neck are so loose that they spread out in all directions and add considerably to the dramatic effect.

. . . . . . . . . . . . . . . . . . .

## INTERMEDIATE EGRET
### *(Egretta intermedia)*

LEFT: **K**nown as plumed egrets in Asia, yellow-billed egrets in Africa and intermediate egrets in Australia, these birds live together quite happily during most of the year. They breed in mixed colonies, roost together at night, and sometimes even share a meal of fish and amphibians. However, at the beginning of each breeding season they temporarily change character, picking fights with each other and generally becoming extremely aggressive and touchy.

. . . . . . . . . . . . . . . . . . .

# CHAPTER SEVEN

# PARENTS AND OFFSPRING

**SCALED QUAIL**
*(Callipepla squamata)*

ALL BIRDS LAY EGGS. *Some lay just one, others produce several enormous clutches every season. Eggs come in a variety of shapes, sizes and colours. Hummingbirds lay the smallest, weighing as little as 0.013 oz (0.37 g). Ostriches lay the largest, at 3 lb 11 oz (1.70 kg) an astonishing 4,500 times heavier. The extinct elephant bird from Madagascar laid eggs which were bigger still — so huge that they weighed the equivalent of two or three of the largest dinosaur eggs.*

*Most eggs are well-camouflaged, their colours and patterns blending in perfectly with the surroundings. But every bird needs a nest or similar safe place in which to lay them.*

*Nests vary greatly in design and size. Woodpeckers excavate holes in trees, while there is a hummingbird that builds a tiny cup-nest no bigger than a thimble, and an eagle that constructs an enormous platform of sticks weighing more than a family-sized car.*

**MALLARD**
*(Anas playtyrhnchos)*

*Some birds spend days, or even weeks, turning and pushing, weaving and trampling intricate constructions together. They build with mud, leaves, twigs and sticks, reeds, moss, feathers, wool and horsehair, as well as with more unexpected items such as string, paper, plastic bags or nails. Other birds prefer to lay their eggs in simple scrapes in the ground, or to balance them on thin branches or precarious cliff ledges. King and emperor penguins simply carry their eggs around on the tops of their feet.*

**YELLOW-BREASTED SUNBIRD**
*(Nectarinia jugularis)*

*Nest sites are usually chosen to provide shelter and protection from predators. Some birds seek protection in numbers by breeding*

in large colonies, others camouflage their nests or hide them. The great Indian hornbill keeps raiders out by blocking the entrance to its nesting hole with mud while the female is trapped inside. A warbler in Australia organises a personal security system by building its own nest alongside a nest of hornets. Skuas, terns and many owls resort to attacking unwelcome intruders themselves.

Some cuckoos prefer to avoid the responsibilities of parenthood altogether by laying their eggs in other birds' nests. Even moorhens sometimes sneak a few of their own eggs into neighbours' nests for safe-keeping.

Once laid, the eggs have to be kept warm if they are to develop properly. Most parent birds incubate their eggs by sitting on them. Hour after hour, they patiently put up with bad weather, buzzing insects and the threat of predators wandering around nearby. The shortest period between laying and hatching is about ten days, but for many birds the incubation period is much longer. An albatross' egg has to be kept warm for ten weeks before it hatches.

Many birds have developed ingenious alternative methods of incubation. The blue-footed booby stands on its eggs, while the megapode bird builds an enormous compost heap of rotting vegetation which generates so much heat that it can bury its eggs inside and, apart from checking the temperature once in a while, leave them alone.

Eggshell is very strong and, when they are ready to hatch, young birds must spend hours or even days chipping and breaking their way out. Some newly hatched chicks are well-developed and born with their eyes open and a coat of downy feathers. They leave the nest and begin to fend for themselves within 24 hours. The chicks of many other species hatch blind and naked and are unable to survive on their own until they are many weeks or months old. It is only the tireless help of their parents that keeps them alive.

**LONG-TAILED TAILORBIRD**
*(Orthotomus sutorius maculicollis)*

## AFRICAN PARADISE FLYCATCHER
### (Terpsiphone viridis)

LEFT: The paradise flycatcher appears to take great pride in its nest. This is built in a shaded, delicate fork of a narrow branch, often overhanging some water. Riverine forests are favourite localities, but thickets, gardens or anywhere else with plenty of vegetation will suffice. The nest itself consists of a shallow cup of bark, roots and grass, neatly bound together with spiders' webs and lined with rootlets. The bird in this picture has a 10 in (25.4 cm) long tail and is a male; the female's tail is much shorter. Both birds share the task of feeding their chicks with insects caught in mid-air.

...................

## BUFF-BREASTED PARADISE KINGFISHER
### (Tanysiptera sylvia)

RIGHT: In the lowland rain forests of north-eastern Queensland and New Guinea, a high-pitched trilling sound can sometimes be heard all day long. This is made during the nesting season by one of the shiest and most beautiful of all the kingfishers. Also known as the white-tailed or racquet-tailed kingfisher, the buff-breasted paradise kingfisher spends most of its time high in the canopy of the forest, feeding on insects and small reptiles. Surprisingly, it breeds very close to the ground, inside a chamber in an active termite nest.

...................

### RUFOUS FANTAIL
#### (Rhipidura rufifrons)

ABOVE: **A**s it flits and flutters around in the foliage or on the ground, the rufous fantail always carries its long tail partly cocked. It is continuously opening it into a fan, waving it from side to side and closing it again. A hyperactive bird, its sudden movements are believed to flush insects into the air. These are snapped up in flight or picked off the foliage as soon as they move. Rufous fantails are popular birds in their native South-east Asia and Australia. They occasionally enter buildings and show a great interest in people, frequently hovering right in front of them. Their neat cup nest is built on the thin, forked branch of a bush or tree and may be used by a breeding pair to produce as many as five broods in a year.

. . . . . . . . . . . . . . . . . . .

### HOATZIN
#### (Opisthocomus hoazin)

RIGHT: **H**oatzins are strange birds. Strict vegetarians, excellent swimmers and terribly smelly, they are possibly related to cuckoos – but more closely resemble domestic chickens. They live along the wooded riverbanks of the Amazon and Orinoco basins, where they build untidy stick nests over the water. The young chicks are naked and look quite helpless, but they habitually leave their nests soon after hatching. They have two hooked claws on the front edge of each wing – just like the prehistoric bird *Archaeopteryx* – which help them to clamber around in the branches nearby. These claws are shed within a few weeks. Adult hoatzins also spend a lot of time clambering among the branches, using their wings for support and balance. They are poor fliers and can barely manage to travel a hundred yards or so before crashing into the vegetation for a rest.

. . . . . . . . . . . . . . . . . . .

### GREAT-SPOTTED WOODPECKER
*(Dendrocopos major)*

LEFT: Great-spotted woodpeckers hammer their strong, straight
bills against tree trunks with such force that it is a wonder their
skulls can absorb the punishment. Scientists have been studying
them in the hope of discovering useful hints for improving the
design of crash helmets worn by motorcyclists. The male and
female woodpeckers work together in excavating their nest-hole.
They prefer dead or decaying trees, but sometimes have to spend
more than two weeks tunnelling into particularly hard wood.
Even then, they may lose the hole to other woodland birds, which
move in as squatters. Great-spotted woodpeckers are common in
many parts of Europe, North Africa and Asia. The bird in this
picture is a male; the red band at the back of his head is missing
in the female. The young bird inside the nest cavity will lose its
red cap when it moults in the autumn.

. . . . . . . . . . . . . . . . . . .

### COMMON FLICKER
*(Colaptes auratus)*

RIGHT: There are several varieties of common flicker. They are
all so different that, at one time, they were considered to be three
distinct species. Active and noisy birds, they belong to the
woodpecker family and are a common sight in the open
woodlands and suburban gardens in parts of North and Central
America. The male proclaims his territory and attracts a mate by
hammering his bill on the side of a tree, or on a tin roof, to make
a drumming sound. The same nest-site is generally used for
several years, but from time to time the male selects a suitable
tree trunk, stump or telegraph pole for a new one – and does most
of the excavation work himself.

. . . . . . . . . . . . . . . . . . .

**CAPE WEAVER**
*(Ploceus capensis)* LEFT
**BAYA WEAVER**
*(Ploceus philippinus)* CENTRE LEFT
**BLACK-HEADED WEAVER**
*(Ploceus melanocephalus)* OPPOSITE

Weavers are the architects of the bird world. Using their bills
and feet to tie knots, they make their nests by weaving grass and
other suitable materials into elaborate, hollow balls. These are
suspended next to one another from branches, reeds or even
telegraph wires, and there may be several-hundred nests hanging
from a single tree. Each species has its own rigid, easily
recognisable design. The baya weaver makes a globular nest,
with a long entrance tube at the bottom to keep out snakes and
other predators; some species build tunnels that are more than
2 ft (60 cm) long. Cape weavers make kidney-shaped chambers
with very short tunnels, while yellow-backed weavers make no
tunnels at all for their relatively simple, ball-shaped nests. Most
true weavers are found in the savannas and forests of Africa,
although there are exceptions. The baya weaver, for example,
lives in south and South-east Asia.

. . . . . . . . . . . . . . . . . . . .

**LONG-TAILED HERMIT**
*(Phaethornis superciliosus)*

BOTTOM RIGHT: The long-tailed hermit is a kind of hummingbird
that lives in the rain forests of Central and South America. It is
an inquisitive little bird that sometimes hovers directly in front of
people in order to have a closer look at them. Its extraordinary
nest is built with mosses and roots bound together with spiders'
webs. The cup holding the eggs is attached to the underside of a
drooping palm leaf and pieces of earth are woven into the long,
conical tail to act as a balance for holding the nest steady.

. . . . . . . . . . . . . . . . . . . .

## BLUE TIT
### *(Parus caeruleus)*

Blue tits are woodland birds that have taken advantage of the many attractions available to them in suburban gardens. They are often the most consistent visitors to bird tables in the winter and will readily nest in artificial boxes in the spring. Nestboxes are designed to resemble holes in trees – although the birds are not too fussy and sometimes use old cans, letter-boxes and a variety of other unlikely cavities. The nest is made of moss, dried grass, dead leaves and bark, the cup itself being lined with hair, feathers, down or wool. Blue tits usually lay up to 12 tiny eggs, although broods have been as large as 19 and, particularly in gardens, are frequently as small as five or six. Hatching is timed to coincide with the greatest abundance of caterpillars, which are the staple diet of the youngsters. The young leave the nest after about three weeks. Only one or two of them survive until the following year. Blue tits are common in Europe and many parts of Asia.

.....................

### EURASIAN EAGLE OWL
### (Bubo bubo)

ABOVE: **E**agle owls generally breed on rocky hillsides, ravines or cliff ledges, although they sometimes make use of the abandoned nests of other birds such as buzzards and eagles. The young owlets leave their nests when they are a little over a month old, but are quite helpless for several more weeks since they are unable to fly and still rely on their parents for food. However, the breeding season is early in the year, so there is plenty of time for the young birds to perfect their hunting skills while food is still abundant. The Eurasian eagle owl is found in Europe and Asia, and has recently extended its range to North Africa.

. . . . . . . . . . . . . . . . . . .

### BARN OWL
### (Tyto alba)

LEFT: **B**arn owls are probably responsible for many ghost stories. In the darkness they appear ghostly white and, in the evening and at night, they can often be seen patrolling low over the ground in churchyards. They add to the spectacle by uttering unearthly screeches and wails, spooky hissing and gargling screams. Barn owls nest in holes in trees and frequently use out-buildings, church towers and other man-made sites. Farmers often place special nesting trays for the owls in their barns; they are welcome birds because they catch pests such as rats and mice. Found on farmland, moors and other open country in Europe, North and South America, Africa, parts of Russia and Asia, and Australia, they are among the world's best-known owls.

. . . . . . . . . . . . . . . . . . .

### SCREECH OWL
### (Otus asio)

RIGHT: **D**ubbed 'feathered wild cats' by many bird watchers, screech owls are fearless when defending their nests. They are small birds, hardly bigger than starlings, but will attack – and sometimes kill – intruders considerably larger than themselves. Found in a variety of habitats, from open woodland and cactus desert to suburban gardens, they occur in many parts of eastern North America. The female lays four or five eggs inside a hole in a tree and, while she incubates them, she is fed by the male. The young birds (such as the one in this picture) leave home when they are a month old but continue to be fed by their parents for another five or six weeks.

. . . . . . . . . . . . . . . . . . .

### OSTRICH
### *(Struthio camelus)*

**O**striches grow up to 9 ft (2.7 m) tall and are famous for being
the largest living birds. They are too big to fly, but are able to run
across the African grasslands at speeds of up to 40 miles (64 km)
per hour. They have a very peculiar breeding system. The male
makes several shallow scrapes in the ground and then leaves his
partner to select one while he mates with up to five other females.
All his 'wives' then lay their huge eggs in the same scrape. The
eggs each measure up to 8 in (20 cm) in length, are equivalent in
volume to about 24 hens' eggs and have a shell strong enough to
support the weight of a man. Initially, there may be as many as
40 eggs in the same nest – but the dominant female selects which
ones to keep. To the human eye, they all look identical, but she
is able to tell the difference by the pore patterns on their plain
white shells. It is in her interests to incubate some of the other
females' eggs because the more there are in the nest, the smaller
the chance of one of her own being taken by a predator. She
therefore selects a clutch of about 20 and rolls the surplus away.
The eggs that are left are incubated at night by the male, while
the more dangerous daytime shift is taken over by the dominant
female, who sometimes rests her neck on the ground to 'hide'
from potential predators. Once the eggs have hatched, the chicks
join the young birds from other nests and, together, they form an
enormous creche which is looked after by one or two adults.

. . . . . . . . . . . . . . . . . . . .

### GREAT-CRESTED GREBE
*(Podiceps cristatus)*

LEFT: Since they are unable to walk easily on land, great-crested grebes build floating nests on the water. These consist of heaps of rotting vegetation anchored among the reeds at the edge of a pond or lake. However, their fluffy and boldly marked chicks spend little time actually in the nest and, soon after hatching, are carried around by their parents. They are fed on insects and fish for nearly three months, and young birds the size of their parents continue to plead for food. Found in many parts of the world, with the exception of the Americas, the great-crested grebe is best known for its elaborate courtship ceremony. This includes a sequence in which both birds rise from the water face-to-face and present each other with water plants.

. . . . . . . . . . . . . . . . . . . . .

### OSPREY
*(Pandion haliaetus)*

ABOVE: An osprey's nest is enormous. Built of sticks, grass and heather, usually on the very top of a pine or spruce tree, it is used year after year and added to at the beginning of each new season. During incubation, the female sits on the eggs while the male feeds her with fish. He then has to feed the whole family while his mate stays with the nestlings, tearing up the food and feeding it to them individually. When the birds are older, both parents provide the food, simply dropping whole fish into the nest. Ospreys breed all over the world, with the exception of South America and Antarctica. Populations in Europe and North America have dwindled seriously due to hunting, egg collecting and the widespread use of chemical pesticides.

. . . . . . . . . . . . . . . . . . . . .

**BLUE-FOOTED BOOBY**
*(Sula nebouxii)*

The term 'booby' comes from the Spanish word 'bobo', meaning
foolish. Blue-footed boobies certainly look comical during
courtship as they parade around in front of their mates, lifting
their vivid blue feet high in the air one after the other. Members
of the gannet family, they live on the Galapagos Islands and
along the western coasts of tropical America. Their courtship
dances also involve pretending to build nests by picking up twigs
and stones and placing them on the ground; these are cleared
away by the females before they lay up to three eggs in the bare
dust. The eggs are incubated by both parents but, once they have
hatched, the male feeds the chicks with fish while the female
looks after them. The male cannot cope alone as the youngsters
grow larger, so eventually the female helps to satisfy their
enormous appetites. Unless food is plentiful, the youngest chicks
usually starve to death because their older siblings are larger and
stronger and steal all the food. The survivors return, two or three
years later, to the same colonies to find their own mates and
breed themselves.

. . . . . . . . . . . . . . . . . . .

### CHINSTRAP PENGUIN
*(Pygoscelis antarctica)*

**C**hinstrap penguins are good climbers. They prefer high, rocky sites for their nests on the islands around Antarctica; these nests are sometimes more than 300 ft (93 m) above sea level. Two eggs are laid in a simple scrape on the ground, which is ringed with just enough pebbles to keep the eggs from rolling over any nearby precipices. The first long incubation period is the responsibility of the female, but thereafter she alternates with the male every two or three days. The principal food of chinstrap penguins is krill and they frequently have to travel as far as 50 miles (80 km) to reach the best hunting grounds. They compete with the great whales for this food source and, since several centuries of intensive whaling have devastated whale populations, penguin numbers have been increasing. Indeed, today there are chinstrap colonies in existence numbering tens or even hundreds of thousands of individuals. The young chinstraps have an astonishing capacity for food and their parents bring them back more than 1 lb (2.2 kg) of krill after each hunting trip. At the end of the breeding season, the adults moult to replace their old feathers – which must be watertight before they can swim – in preparation for a long winter at sea.

. . . . . . . . . . . . . . . . . . . .

### REED WARBLER
*(Acrocephalus scirpaceus)*

LEFT: **A** reed warbler's nest seems to be supported by friction alone. It is woven around several living reed stems, over shallow water, but has very little support underneath. The cup of grass is particularly deep, and this prevents the eggs or young from being tossed out when the reeds bend over in the wind. Old nests are often dismantled to make new ones, and the birds may even steal good-looking material from the nests of their neighbours. The young warblers, which are fed on insects by both their parents, always seem to be in a hurry to leave home. They do so after as little as ten days and, although it is a further week before they can fly, they are adept at moving about on the reed stems. Breeding in Europe and western Asia, reed warblers are favourite victims of the cuckoo, which removes one of their eggs and replaces it with one of its own.

. . . . . . . . . . . . . . . . . . . .

### GALAH
*(Cacatua roseicapilla)*

ABOVE: **T**he elegant pink- and grey-coloured galah, otherwise known as the goolie, or willie-willock, is one of the commonest parrots in Australia. A galah's nest, which is usually built in a hollow tree, has two unusual and very distinctive features. The bark is typically stripped from around its entrance, and the nest-hollow is lined with green eucalyptus leaves and twigs. Like many other members of the parrot family, galahs are extremely noisy birds and prefer the rowdy company of others to a quiet life alone. They tend to show off and perform antics when they are together.

. . . . . . . . . . . . . . . . . . .

### BLACK-BROWED ALBATROSS
*(Diomedea melanophris)*

ABOVE: **A** typical black-browed albatross colony, on a sub-Antarctic island, is wet and muddy. The birds therefore build tall nests of packed soil and grass to keep their eggs and chicks dry. With a little renovation at the beginning of each season, these columnar nests last for many years. They have a very small circumference and a large chick perched on the top is a comical sight. Outside the breeding season, black-browed albatrosses, or mollymawks as they are often called, patrol the southern oceans between Antarctica and Australia, Africa and South America, following trawlers or hunting for krill, squid and fish.

. . . . . . . . . . . . . . . . . . .

### ROYAL ALBATROSS
*(Diomedia epomophora)*

RIGHT: **S**ince they can live to be 50 years old, royal albatrosses seem to be in no hurry to start breeding. They remain free and single, gliding over the southern seas, for seven or eight years before looking for a suitable mate. Then the two birds 'go steady' for a year before settling down together. It is an important decision, because they pair for life. The male is usually the first to appear at their colony on one of the islands around New Zealand, although the female often follows only a few hours later. Their breeding season is a particularly long one: from egg-laying to the departure of the chick takes more than ten months.

. . . . . . . . . . . . . . . . . . .

### HOOPOE
### *(Upupa epops)*

**H**oopoes may be strikingly beautiful birds but they are also terribly smelly. They secrete a foul-smelling substance from their preen glands and have a nasty habit of spraying everything with excreta whenever they are frightened. Their nest-sites are, not surprisingly, rather fetid. They like the entrance to be so narrow that they have to squeeze themselves inside, but will make do with a variety of locations, including holes in trees, termite-mounds, old buildings, dry-stone walls and gaps between rocks. The female lays up to nine eggs (fewer in the tropics) in the scantily lined nest and, while she incubates them, she is fed by her mate. For the first few days after hatching, she stays with the youngsters while he finds sufficient food for the whole family. Later on, she joins him in his hectic search for insects, earthworms, frogs, lizards and other small animals. Hoopoes are a familiar sight in gardens, orchards and other open country with scattered trees in many parts of Europe, Asia and Africa. As their name suggests, they have a low-pitched, dove-like 'hoop-hoop-hoop' call.

. . . . . . . . . . . . . . . . . . . .

### WHISKERED TERN
#### (Chlidonias hybrida)

LEFT: **W**hiskered terns breed in small, loose colonies. Although they may occasionally use the old nests of other waterbirds, they usually build their own. The nests consist of piles of grass or rushes which are either floating or anchored to nearby aquatic plants. These birds are also known as marsh terns and occur virtually worldwide, except for the Americas, in lakes, swamps, rivers and brackish lagoons. They have a varied diet, ranging from moths and flying ants to tadpoles and small fish. Flying with slow wingbeats into the wind, they capture insects in flight or other prey by plunge-diving or by picking them off the surface of the water.

. . . . . . . . . . . . . . . . . . . .

### WHITE TERN
#### (Gygis alba)

ABOVE AND BELOW: **T**he white tern lays its single egg directly on to a tree branch. Precariously balanced, it is in constant danger of being knocked to the ground. The newly hatched chick also has balancing problems, but it has enormous, rather comical, hooked feet for hanging on to its unsafe perch. It patiently sits there for several weeks, clinging to the branch on which it hatched and waiting for its parents to bring it fish. When fully fledged, white terns are unmistakable and lovely birds, snow white all over except for their jet-black bills and eyes and slate-blue legs. Also known as fairy terns, they breed on many tropical and sub-tropical islands in the Atlantic, Pacific and Indian Oceans.

. . . . . . . . . . . . . . . . . . . .

## CARMINE BEE-EATER
### *(Merops nubicus)*

A one-year-old bee-eater usually attaches itself to an older breeding pair as a 'nanny'. It helps to excavate the nest, feed the young and carry out other duties. It may be learning the necessary techniques in preparation for its own efforts the following year. Carmine bee-eaters excavate their nesting burrows in the steep banks of river valleys throughout much of Africa. They breed in large colonies, some of which have several-thousand burrows, each about 6 ft (1.8 m) long. The nests are not lined, but the eggs soon get fouled with faeces and buried in regurgitated pellets and insect remains. The parents and helpers bring back so many flying insects, such as beetles and grasshoppers, that after fledging the chicks are overweight and often bigger than the adults. The birds in this picture are northern carmine bee-eaters which were photographed in Cameroon, West Africa; the southern race lacks their greenish throats.

. . . . . . . . . . . . . . . . . . . . .

# Picture Credits

. . . . . . . . . . . . . . . . . . .

6: Frieder Sauer/Bruce Coleman; Wayne Lynch/Bryan and Cherry Alexander Photography; Dennis Avon/Ardea; Robert and Linda Mitchell; Armstrong/Zefa. 7: Zefa. 8: M. C. Wilkes/Aquila; Geoff Dore/Bruce Coleman. 9: C. Carvalho/Frank Lane – Geoff Dore/Bruce Coleman; Stephen Dalton/NHPA. 10: Hans Reinhard/Bruce Coleman; Philip Perry/Frank Lane. 11: Stephen Dalton/NHPA – W. Wisniewski/Okapia. 12/13: Jean-Philippe Varin/Jacana; Joseph van Wormer/Bruce Coleman; A. Greensmith/Ardea. 14/15: Fred Bruemmer/Okapia. 16: Mark Carwardine/Biotica. 17: Tony Howard/NHPA. 18/19: Peter Davey/Bruce Coleman. 20/21: S. Nielsen/Bruce Coleman – Manfred Danegger/NHPA. 22: Jen and Des Bartlett/Bruce Coleman. 23: John Shaw/NHPA. 24/25: Ralph and Daphne Keller/NHPA – Hellio and Van Ingen/NHPA. 26: P. Doherty/Aquila; Clem Haagner/Ardea; Eric and David Hosking. 27: Mark Carwardine/Biotica. 28/29: Robert and Linda Mitchell – Mark Carwardine/Biotica. 30: Tony Howard/NHPA. 31: R. T. Peterson/Zefa; Fred Winner/Jacana. 32/33: Mark Carwardine/Biotica. 34/35: Orion Press/NHPA. 36: G. K. Brown/Ardea. 37: Jean-Paul Ferrero/Ardea. 38/39: Michael Fogden. 40: Gunter Ziesler/Bruce Coleman. 41: R. J. Erwin/NHPA. 42/43: Jaunet/Jacana – Haroldo Palo Jr./NHPA. 44/45: Jean-Paul Ferrero/Ardea. 46: Peter Steyn/Ardea; S. Cordier/Jacana. 47: Reser/Zefa; Nigel Dennis/NHPA; Robert and Linda Mitchell. 48: Mark Carwardine/Biotica. 49: Francisco Erize/Bruce Coleman. 50: T. Dressler/Okapia. 51: Fritz Polking/Okapia. 52/53: Eric and David Hosking – Frank Lane. 54: W. Layer/Zefa. 55: Stephen Dalton/NHPA. 56: Michael Leach/NHPA; Jeff Foott/Okapia; Francois Gohier/Jacana. 57: Andy Purcell/Bruce Coleman. 58/59: Fritz Polking/Okapia. 60: Sullivan and Rogers/Bruce Coleman. 61: Wayne Lankinen/Aquila. 62/63: John Shaw/NHPA – Mike Wilkes/Aquila. 64: Michael Leach/NHPA. 65: Mark Carwardine/Biotica. 66: Mark Carwardine/Biotica. 67: NHPA. 68: Peter Steyn/Ardea; Kenneth W. Fink/Ardea – Mark Carwardine/Biotica. 69: Lothar Lenz/Okapia; Michael Fogden. 70/71: Jane Burton/Bruce Coleman. 72/73: Nigel Dennis/NHPA – Robert and Linda Mitchell. 74: Frans Lanting/Bruce Coleman. 75: Kenneth W. Fink/Ardea; Mark Carwardine/Biotica. 76: U. Mohrke/Okapia; Bernd Thies/Bruce Coleman. 77: Nigel Dennis/NHPA. 78: Th. Hofmann/Okapia; A. R. Hamblin/Frank Lane. 79: Manfred Danegger/NHPA; Fred Winner/Jacana. 80: M. Morcombe/NHPA. 81: Raimund Cramm/Okapia. 82/83: Robert and Linda Mitchell – A. Gandolfi/Jacana. 84: Michael Fogden. 85: J-M Labat/Jacana. 86/87: John E. Swedberg/Ardea – Dieter and Mary Plage/Bruce Coleman. 88: Hellio and Van Ingen/NHPA. 89: Brian Gadsby; Alan Barnes/APB Photographics; L. Campbell/NHPA. 90: Manfred Danegger/NHPA. 91: Joe McDonald/Okapia. 92: Stephen Dalton/NHPA. 93: Mark Carwardine/Biotica. 94/95: B. and C. Calhoun/Bruce Coleman – Wardene Weisser/Ardea. 96/97: Peter Johnson/NHPA; W. Wisniewski/Okapia. 98: Manfred Danegger/NHPA. 99: Wayne Lankinen/Aquila. 100: Mike Price/Bruce Coleman – Mark Carwardine/Biotica; John Shaw/NHPA. 101: Frans Lanting/Bruce Coleman. 102/103: A. R. Hamblin/Frank Lane – Martin W. Grosnick/Ardea. 104: James H. Carmichael Jr./NHPA. 105: Joanna van Gruisen/Ardea. 106/107: Roger Tidman/NHPA – M. Grey/NHPA. 108: Zefa – Stephen Dalton/NHPA. 109: Zefa; N. G. Blake/Bruce Coleman – Eric and David Hosking; W. Wisniewski/Frank Lane – S. Cordier/Jacana; Gunter Ziesler/Bruce Coleman. 110: John Shaw/NHPA. 111: Michael Leach/NHPA – Haroldo Palo Jr./NHPA; Roger Tidman/NHPA. 112/113: J-M Labat/Jacana – Philippa Scott/NHPA. 114: Michael Fogden. 115: W. Wisniewski/Okapia. 116/117: Mark Carwardine/Biotica. 118: Steven Kaufman/Bruce Coleman – Tsutomu Tsutsui/Bruce Coleman; Steven Kaufman/Bruce Coleman. 119: Francois Gohier/Jacana. 120/121: T. and P. Gardner/Frank Lane – S. Cordier/Jacana. 122: R. Glover/Aquila. 123: Uwe Walz/Okapia; Mark Carwardine/Biotica. 124: Wayne Lankinen/Aquila – Nigel Dennis/NHPA; Gunter Ziesler/Bruce Coleman. 125: Rolf Bender/Okapia. 126: Robert and Linda Mitchell; Scott Nielsen/Bruce Coleman; Robert and Linda Mitchell. 127: Robert and Linda Mitchell. 128: Peter Steyn/Ardea. 129: C. B. and D. W. Frith/Bruce Coleman. 130: M. Morcombe/NHPA. 131: A. Warren/Ardea. 132: Zefa. 133: Wayne Lankinen/Aquila. 134: Peter Johnson/NHPA; Robert and Linda Mitchell; Gunter Ziesler/Bruce Coleman. 135: J-M Labat/Jacana. 136/137: Jean-Philippe Varin/Jacana – H. P. Laub/Okapia. 138: Axel/Jacana – B. Roth/Okapia. 139: Robert and Linda Mitchell. 140/141: Jen and Des Bartlett/Bruce Coleman; Christian Zuber/Bruce Coleman. 142: Manfred Danegger/NHPA. 143: Robert and Linda Mitchell. 144/145: Francois Gohier/Ardea; Hans D. Dossenbach/Ardea. 146/147: C. Carvalho/Frank Lane; Francois Gohier/Jacana. 148: Les Baker/Aquila. 149: Jean-Paul Ferrero/Ardea. 150: Peter Steyn/Ardea. 151: Jean-Paul Ferrero/Ardea. 152/153: Peter Steyn/Ardea – Francois Gohier/Jacana. 154/155: Hellio and Van Ingen/NHPA – Mark Carwardine/Biotica. 156/157: Michael Fogden.

Endpapers: Zefa; C. Carvalho/Frank Lane; Martin Wendler/NHPA; Nigel Dennis/NHPA; Eric and David Hosking; Fritz Polking/Frank Lane.

# INDEX

**Editorial Assistance**
Index by Peter Moloney.

**Author's Acknowledgments**
Mark Carwardine wishes to thank editor Krystyna Mayer for her enthusiasm, patience and hard work; Doreen Montgomery for her invaluable support, as always; Richard Lewis for so many good ideas and comments; David Bellamy for all his help and encouragement over the years; and Deborah Taylor for being so understanding, yet again.